# A Journey to the Other side of LIFE ™

# A Journey to the other side of LIFE ™

**Understanding Your Emotions
in the Pursuit of
Love, Healing, Freedom and Peace**

# KEVIN LANE TURNER

*Ashley Down Publishing Co.*

Dallas

FIRST EDITION

Editor: Ginger Dennis
Cover design: Kent Robbins Illustration and Hanson Design
Photography: Bill Hurst
Illustrations: Illustrations were created by Ashley Down Publishing Co., using computer generated Click Art by T-Maker, 1390 Villa St., Mountain View, CA 94041

**Publisher's Cataloging in Publication**
*(Prepared by Quality Books Inc.)*
Turner, Kevin Lane. 1957–
    A journey to the other side of life: understanding your emotions in the pursuit of love, healing, freedom, and peace / Kevin Lane Turner. —1st ed.
    p. cm.
    Includes index.
    Library of Congress Cataloging Number — 94-068209
    ISBN 1-886122-73-3
    1. Emotions--Popular works. I. Title
BF561.T87 1995                    152.4
                                          QBI94-21341

Printed in the United States of America

95  96 97 98 99 / 10  9 8 7 6 5 4 3 2 1

With the exception of the author's personal stories, the names and the circumstances in this book have been fictionalized and represent a composite of the clientele that the author has worked with.

## Dedicated to:

*The silent sufferers of emotional fear, wounding and pain;*
*those who know and live with the destructive and painful*
*emotional habits day-in and day-out.*
*May your heart be healed, made whole, and set free:*
*free to live and love in peace.*

If unavailable in local bookstores, additional copies of this and other publications by Kevin Lane Turner may be purchased by writing or calling the publisher at:

Ashley Down Publishing Company
14999 Preston Rd, Suite D212-222
Dallas, TX 75240-7811
(214) 233-9998

A portion of the proceeds from the sales of this book are being distributed to the following charitable organizations:
Children's Medical Center of Dallas
A Weekend to Wipe Out Cancer
Scottish Rite Hospitals for Children
Spina Bifida Association of America

# Publisher's Note

The message within *A Journey to the Other Side of Life* is very different from that with which we are familiar. This book causes us to shift the way we read, think and perceive. Purposefully, Kevin Lane Turner's writing style is different from a traditional writing style.

As you read *A Journey to the Other Side of Life* you will notice repetition within the book. This is done with a purpose. The purpose is to encourage us to shift the way we think. The focus of this volume is entirely emotional (most reading is intellectually focused). This book has been written from an emotional perspective. Unless you have experienced this shift in thinking and perception beforehand, initially you may find some ideas within the book hard to grasp, or at the very least, different. This is because most of us are trained to think and perceive from a physical, mental or even spiritual frame of mind. We are not taught to think and perceive from an emotional perspective. Mr. Turner helps us accomplish this shift in thinking as we read this volume.

Consequently, as you are reading *A Journey to the Other Side of Life* you may sometimes think that your mind is playing tricks on you. Just remember that, yes, you have read or seen that idea before. It is there to get you to stop, think and consider a completely different approach and focus to your life, your relationships, and your feelings.

Because of the uniqueness of the message, you may find yourself coming across some terms that are unfamiliar to you. An excellent glossary is provided for your convenience in the back of this book. Also, for the reader's convenience, three indexes follow the book: an illustration index, a Bible verse index, and a word index.

# Professional Acknowledgements

Many people have contributed to the writing and publication of this book. I must express acknowledgment for those who have contributed to make this book possible.

First, I wish to thank my wife Mary. Your long hours and hard work have made all of this possible.

Second, a special thanks to our editor, Ginger Dennis. Your help with the manuscript was invaluable. You took a rough work and gave it polish. This book would not be in its present form without you. Thanks!

Third, a special thanks to Kent Robbins for taking an idea and bringing it to life (the cover art work).

I also wish to thank those who took the time to read through and critique the manuscript. Your input helped us see what we could not see on our own:

1. Matthew Ammon
2. Lorie Ammon
3. Jeff Boyd
4. Nora Curlett
5. Mary Davis
6. Ginger Dennis
7. Carol Fasulo
8. Meagon Fletcher
9. Dennis Hassell
10. Carol Irwin
11. Jennifer Jackson
12. Debbie Landa
13. Pamela Lorton
14. David Mathews
15. Suzanne Mathews
16. Kristie Monroe
17. Linda Moody
18. Barry Moore
19. Cheryl Scruggs
20. Diane Walker
21. Dr. Gerald Walters

Finally, a special thanks to all of those who came through our counseling/life-improvement process and in so doing, validated and verified the principles we espouse in this book.

# Personal Acknowledgements

Realizing that no man or woman is an island, it would be foolish of me to assume full responsibility for what I know and have discovered about the emotions encased within us all. Therefore, in giving credit where credit is due, I can not share the ideas within this book without acknowledging the mark others have left on my life. For it is the mark of others that has shaped my thinking and formulated my approach to life.

I first wish to thank and acknowledge my Creator. For me, you truly are my Lord. But more than that, you are and have been my closest companion and friend. Thank you for giving me a new beginning emotionally, as well as spiritually.

To my wife, Mary, thank you for being who you are. You are my best friend. You have taught me acceptance, commitment, and the importance of human companionship and teamwork.

A special thanks to my children—Dawson, Hudson, Jonathan, George, Quip and Maria—for teaching me humility, patience and love.

Also, I wish to thank my wife and children collectively—*The Turner Family Machine.* We worked as a team on the production of this book. It could not have been done without you. You are the greatest!

Thank you Mother. You taught me to be bold, to dream, and to believe in myself; those are the greatest gifts a mother could give her child.

Thank you Dad. You taught me kindness, the value of money, and the importance of honesty and integrity.

Thank you Barbara Phillips for being a friendly refuge during some turbulent times in my teen years.

Thank you J.C. Mitchell for steering me to the next avenue in my life during my college years.

Thank you Billy Cline for sacrificially giving of yourself and your time into my life for over two years. I trust the Heavens will one day say that it was a good investment.

Thank you Vance and Irene Harris. You took me in as one of your own and taught me many valuable lessons during my early adult years. You gave me and allowed me to feel a sense of family.

Thank you Homer and Elsie Dyer. You too took me in as one of your own. Your love and acceptance will always be treasured.

Thank you Gray Allison. You accepted someone who did not fit a ministerial standard (no tie and long hair!) and you led me to learn of a man who greatly changed my approach to life—George Muller.

Thank you Gary Miller for the inspiriation of your savvy and sense for business.

Thank you Bill and Martha Radeck. Like others, you took me in. Yet by this time, I had a family and you took us all in. Thank you.

Thank you Adelaide Busey. You too took my family in as we resumed my graduate school studies. Thank you too, for passing on to me one of my greatest lessons—"pass it on." I have and I do!

Thank you Lanny Elmore. You believed in me when few others did.

Thank you Scottie Ashley. Your belief and acceptance of me gave me the self-confidence to follow what God birthed in my heart, the by-product of which is our counseling service and now, this book.

I also wish to thank Gary Hainey and Richard Smith. You believed in me in more ways than one. I will always be grateful.

Thank you Allen and Molly Nance. Thank you for always pursuing our friendship. You truly are the greatest friends a couple could have.

Thank you Daron Day for giving me the original idea for the wounded tree.

Thank you Richard Hicks. Your friendship and example gave me the ability to express my love verbally and physically to others around me without the fear of losing my manhood.

Thank your Brad Burns. Your quiet compassion and your life's example gave me hope for my family and our future generations.

Thank you Terry Moore. You broke down my barriers of fear and self-preservation with constant words of "I love you."

A special thanks to four men who shaped my young adult life, whom I probably will not get to meet until we meet in Heaven: George Muller, Hudson Taylor, Dawson Trotman and Billy Graham. Thank you for your examples of humility and godliness.

Also, my personal acknowledgements would be incomplete if I were to fail to thank the countless people who have come through our counseling/life-improvement process. In so doing, your changed lives have confirmed and validated the emotionally-focused principles we espouse and live by, some of which are explained in this book.

# CONTENTS

# Part III
# The Other Side of Life

# Author's Note

This book is the culmination of almost twenty years of work, research and practice. It is a descriptive *understanding* of how our feelings and emotions, our *emotional*-self, work. It is *not* a book designed to give the "how-to's" for accomplishing emotional love, healing, freedom and peace. To do this would take several volumes.

*A Journey to the Other Side of Life* is the first in a series of books which detail and describe an *emotionally focused* approach, or Journey, into *emotional* healing, life-improvement and change. This book is the first step in the Journey toward a *shift* in perception. The others will follow in the near future. The subsequent volumes will explain the steps or "how to's."

This book is designed to help us better *understand* our feelings, fears and emotions. It answers many of the "whys" which you and I sometimes struggle with when it comes to our feelings and fears. Understanding ourselves, who we are and why we feel and behave the way we do, is the first step toward letting go of the past and moving on into your present and future. This book helps with this understanding.

My goal with this volume is twofold. My first goal is not to obtain more counseling or build a larger organization. I do not particularly want or need more counseling (I do not wish to have more of my time taken away from my wife and my children). However, I do have a desire to see a greater number of people become emotionally whole, healed, free and at peace than could possibly be experienced through one-to-one counseling; this is my first goal.

My second goal for writing this book is my primary goal. It is to give you, the reader, a greater understanding into *why* you *do* what you do, *say* what you say, *feel* what you feel, and *think* what you think. Please write (in care of the publisher) and let me know if I have accomplished my goal. I would like to hear from you.

Kevin

# Preface

$\mathcal{W}$e are living in an age of lost identities and purposes. Many of us roam the earth in search of who we are and why we are here. In pursuit of our own emotional happiness, peace and identity, many of us have emotionally abandoned the essence of life. Many of us have abandoned our homes. Many of us have abandoned our children and our children's children. Many of us have abandoned ourselves.

Technology is increasing. Life's physical and scientific questions are now being answered faster than the questions themselves are being asked. But when it comes to the emotions we feel, many questions remain unanswered. We are living in a time of emotional confusion, loneliness, pain and fear. Although we are discovering technological answers, we are living in an age that has given us very few *emotional* answers. We are living in an emotional bog. However, I believe this is changing.

Because of the heightened rush with technological advances and the seemingly digressed state of relationships and societal life, I believe the world is approaching an apex. Many of us recognize the need for our *emotional* lives to "catch up" with our technological lives. I believe this realization will lead us into an age of spiritual and emotional discovery and renewal. I believe we are approaching an age of emotional and spiritual *enlighten-*

*ment.* It will be a time of understanding. Men and women will seek to move into a greater state of *heart-based* understanding of themselves, their Creator and others around them. In the years ahead, many will seek to grow into a greater awareness of self. We will grow into a greater understanding of our *heart-nature*, our *emotional*-self. We will grow and discover who we are, why we are here, and where we are going.

Technology has not provided us with the answers we seek for our *emotional*-self. Nor has psychiatry provided those answers. However, I believe the day is fast approaching when those answers will come. The answers will reveal to us the mysteries of our heart, our *emotional*-self. In business, government, life and personal relationships, society will search for ways to move away from bickering and battles, and into an age of relational peace and participation.

In the coming age, masses of people will lay down the traditional tools for emotional gratification: money and materialism, politics and performance. Many will desire a higher dimension to their lives. We will pick up the mantel of *self-discovery* and *heart-based* living (this is not to be confused with self-centered living). We will seek to pursue relationships and jobs that will cause our lives to *count* for something—something with more meaning, something more than social, material or political advances. Many of us will seek to brand our mark on the hearts of people, and on the heart of society. We will want our lives to count for good.

Before now, our inner pain and emptiness has caused us to live in the past, bogged down and preoccupied by past wounding, fear and the pain of unfulfilled hopes, dreams and expectations. Now it is time to focus on where we are heading for the remainder of our lives, for ourselves, for our children, and for our children's children.

Many of us are not even aware that our emptiness and dissatisfaction with life, or our difficulty with relationships, are directly connected and related to negative, fearful and wounded emotions from our past. Over the years we suppress, oppress, deny and even forget about the pain and wounding. But their effects on our heart, mind and life stay with us and remain throughout our lives. That is, they stay with us until we face them and change the behavioral habit patterns they trigger within us.

I believe the ideas espoused in this book, when acted upon, will help accomplish this task. This book offers a radically different approach to an age-old dilemma and struggle. The struggle has been to understand who we are and why we feel and behave the way we do.

*A Journey to the Other Side of Life* describes an *emotional* approach for the emotional issues we face. This is different from what has been available to many of us before now. This book addresses the difficulty many people face when it comes to genuine healing, freedom, peace and behavioral habit change. It gives clarity and understanding as to *how* our feelings and emotions function. This book is *emotionally* focused, not psychologically, spiritually, or physically focused (this concept is explained in detail within the book). When we use an *emotional* approach, we do not attempt to understand nor heal our emotions with mental tools (psychology), spiritual tools, or physical tools (medicine or exercise). Instead, we incorporate *emotionally* based tools in the healing and life-improvement process.

Consequently, this book is about a *shift* in perception. We perceive with our minds. We perceive with our spirits. We perceive with our bodies. However, we rarely perceive with our hearts. Instead, we remain distant and out of touch with our hearts, our *emotional*-self. Isn't it time for us to be in touch with our hearts? Life is too short. We have already missed so much because of a wrong perception.

I invite you to come with me on a Journey. If you will enter this Journey, you too will experience a *shift* in perception. Life will blossom. This book introduces us to this *shift*.

So for now, let's enter a Journey, a Journey to a new way of perceiving—A Journey to the Other Side of Life.

# AN INTRODUCTION

## *Foreign Lands,*
## *Filled with Strangers*

 *I* can remember being happy, feeling good about myself and enjoying life.

I remember images of God dropping a rope ladder down from Heaven and letting me climb up to be with Him. I always wanted to go to Heaven and be with Him. For some unexplained reason, I felt a closeness—but it wasn't enough. An unfathomable longing accompanied my heart. I wanted more than images, prayers and songs. I wanted to touch Him, be next to Him and talk with Him. So, I did.

I was happy.

I remember following behind my father on my tricycle as he mowed our yard. The smell of the freshly cut grass seemed to propel my mind while my body and tricycle struggled to keep up with him. The wheels of my tricycle would get stuck in the wet grass. So I would just stop and wait for him to mow another lap and come back around, and I would follow again. As my father rounded the curve and mowed toward his waiting son, he would look me in the eye and smile. His smile was so warm and personable. It filled his whole countenance. My father could smile

7

with his eyes. He always had the most comforting smile of approval and acceptance. I felt so fortunate to have him as my father. "No one else could be as lucky as me," I felt.

I remember going to the rodeo, watching TV westerns, and playing cowboys, as a family—just my mother, my father, and me. These were family things. We were a team. We did things together. I seemed to get a new cowboy outfit every year. I remember the days my father and I had shoot-outs. They were always at the Turner Corral. For some unknown reason, I always won. He always died. Often, we both were shot. My victory had to come with some measure of travail!

I remember the anticipation of my mother's arrival home from work each weekday. I would hide, listening for her familiar words, "Where is Kevin?" as she began her search for me. The fun and exhilaration of the suspense while sitting in the hall closet were more than my little body could bear. It was hard to sit in that dark cubicle alone and remain silent while she searched the house for me. Sometimes, when my little heart could not stand it any longer, I would burst out of that closet. Most of the time, however, my mother would find me. She would surprisingly open the closet door and we would both let out a yell and embrace in pretended relief.

My mother always found me. I always hid in the same closet, day after day. How did she always know where to look? I didn't know! But it was fun. I felt good about myself. It felt good to be loved, missed and sought after. She made me feel very special and important.

I often remember sneaking off with my father to the store and buying a pint of my favorite treat—chocolate milk. The fun was in the fact that it was a secret. It was our secret. No one was to know, especially my mother. It was a secret. In retrospect, Mother probably could have cared less. But that wasn't the point. The secretiveness was suspenseful and fun.

I remember watching the very first episode of *The Beverly Hillbillies* television show. My father's laughter filled the room.

This alone was enough to make me happy. Seeing him happy made me happy. Life was simple, but fun and enjoyable.

I remember Christmases and birthdays—mine, to be more precise. As an only child, I was always showered with an over-abundance of toys and fun things. It was incredible. A new train set came every Christmas.

My birthday parties were big events too. The whole neighborhood seemed to show up. Pictures from that period seem to attest to this. Life was very enjoyable. There was a lot of love and fun and "familiness."

I remember getting my first bicycle, a twenty-inch *Western Flyer*. It was red and accompanied by more bells and whistles than most cars (in my mind anyway). It came at Christmas time of my fifth year.

Little did I know that the red, twenty-inch, *Western Flyer* would soon stand as a symbol of what once was. There was no way I could have known that the bicycle's presence would implant the pain more firmly in my heart as it caused me to remember the past joys while I struggled to cope with the present realities.

During my fifth year, for some incomprehensible reason, my parents split apart, divorced. Life as I knew it was stolen from me. My world was shattered. An incredible wave of fear, uncertainty and loneliness swept into my being. I had been forced to leave a very safe, familiar environment and was thrust into a foreign land, not only physically, but *emotionally* as well. The divorce uprooted us from the place I knew as home. My mother and I, in a car pulling a rental trailer, moved to my grandmother's house. The drive took us two days. My father, I would later learn, moved to his parents' home. Everything about this experience was cold, dark and foreign. We even arrived at our destination in the dark. I had to sleep in a foreign place and live in a foreign house. The home, bedroom, yard, neighbors—everything I was familiar with—were gone. For some hard to understand reason, I was forced to leave my world and enter a new, completely different world.  It was a world filled with strangers. Most of them, I would later learn, were relatives.  But they were strangers to me.  My little mind could not remember having met many of them before this time.  If I had, we had not been around one another very much.  The strangers surely were not as close to me as the friends and neighbors had been back in my old neighborhood.  We had seen one another everyday.  They were my friends and family.  These new strangers were not.

Three things stand out about this time in my life:

First, the physical move from my friendly, comfortable home environment to a foreign land filled with strangers;

Second, in order to be with my father, I had to go and stay in another foreign land filled with still other strangers;

Third, while in these new, dark foreign lands, I had to enter the first grade—yet a third foreign land filled with strangers.

Several months after moving with my mother to the first foreign land filled with strangers, I was sent away to spend the summer with my father.  It turned out to be a second foreign land filled with strangers.  But this one caught my five–year–old heart off balance.  It was starkly different from the first one.  The first one existed within the hustle, bustle and activity of a large metropolitan city.  This second place was in a wilderness, ten miles from the nearest town (a town of only a few hundred inhabitants).  The absolute loneliness was mortifying.  In both places I felt like baggage—something in the way, an inconvenience for others.  But with this second place, that feeling was compounded. I felt like an unwanted obligation to those who were responsible for my well-being during those summer days.  In hindsight, I am sure the feeling would have been the same with both environments.  The difference between the two was that my mother was physically around me much more when I was in her environment than my father was when I was in his.

While I stayed with my father that first summer after their divorce, he worked all day, six days a week.  He was up before the sun and did not come home until after dark.  And then, he was too tired to play. Often he was gone when I would awaken in the mornings. So for the most part, throughout the summer, I rarely saw my father. Consequently, I spent my days being taken care of by strangers. At least that is what it felt like to me. They were my grandparents and relatives. But to a child of five, they were strangers. We had not played together, shared together or laughed together during my first five years. My family had lived a full day's drive from these relatives. So how could they be anything but strangers? Friends and family are supposed to have commonly shared experiences with one another. We hadn't shared anything together.

I had my red, twenty-inch *Western Flyer* with me that summer. Since the entire place consisted of loose sandy dirt (there were no paved streets out in the country), it was too much of an effort to ride my bike. Besides, the mere sight of it always made me remember my past life: my life before the pain, my life before the move, my life before my parents' divorce. So I worked hard to keep that red bike out of my sight. But it was difficult. It seemed to turn up everywhere as a constant reminder of a bygone life. This thought, in itself, brought me intense pain.

I remember one day when I was playing in the road with my favorite toy truck. It was a county dirt road that ran by my grandparents' house. I remember my grandfather yelling for me to get out of the road. A pickup truck was fast approaching. Fear paralyzed me. The truck was barreling toward me. But I could not seem to get out of that road fast enough. I was trying to pick up my toy truck. I could not bear the thought of losing it. While my eyes were riveted on the approaching truck, my hands fumbled for a clean grasp of my toy truck. At the same time, my grandfather was coming towards me, yelling for me to get out of the road. His voice was incredibly deep and intimidating. He could have commanded armies. I barely made it out of the road in time. But I did make it and with my toy truck. However, my grandfather was not pleased. I am not sure which scared me the most, the oncoming truck or my grandfather.

A third foreign land filled with strangers was thrust upon me when I returned to my mother after the summer's stay with my father. I entered my first year of school. It was traumatic to say the least. I remember crying and clinging. I clung to my mother in the classroom on that first day. In six short months I had been swept away from my familiar environment and into not one, but two foreign lands filled with strangers. Now, I found myself in yet a third foreign land filled with strangers. Except this time, there would be *no* familiar faces around me—none. In the first two foreign lands, one of my parents had always been somewhere nearby—not in this new land. I'll never forget that first day of school. My mother pulled my clutching arms away from her body and walked out of the room. The feelings of abandonment were intense. Years later I would learn that this and other similar scenes tore at my mother's heart as well.

So began my Journey into an altered life. It was one that would, for years, be accompanied by hurt, pain, fear, loneliness, rejection and more. It altered what I *did*, what I *said*, how I *felt*, what I *thought*, and how I interacted with life and society.

Without realizing it, I had entered into what I now know as *the wounded life*. Life as I had known it, and grown accustomed to, came to an abrupt end. This new life brought with it an on-slaught of negative feelings, fears and emotions. I felt alone in these feelings. I was convinced I was alone. I had entered into a life of emotional wounding. This new life would, in time, alter my behavior. Mentally, verbally, physically and emotionally, my behavior changed—for the worse.

My elementary years were tough. My grades were poor. We moved a lot. I wanted to die. Even the God I had felt so close to as a younger child had left me, or so it felt. I remember staring out of the classroom into the outside world. The teacher was teaching. I was feeling numb, wishing I could run away to some far away place. I did not know where. Just somewhere where things would feel good again. It never happened.

Friendships were hard to maintain. As soon as we settled into a new place and friendships began to develop, we would move. It was tough. This, combined with the natural cruelty that seems to accompany childhood peer groups who are secure in their environments, caused me to turn inward just to protect myself from more pain. At least I turned inward *emotionally*.

Outwardly however, I projected a front, an image of what I wanted others to see and how I wanted others to perceive me. Sometimes it worked. Often, it did not. This is what wounding did to me. Wounding does this to all of us. It causes us to alter our behavior—anything to protect our hearts from further pain.

The loneliness stayed with me through junior high and on into high school. I assumed that everyone else was growing up in a perfect, unconditionally loving and accepting environment. Beaver did. Opie, even without his mother, did too. So I concluded that surely everyone around me was growing up in a happy, fulfilling environment as well. They sure looked as though they were.

It wasn't until early adulthood that I learned that I had company. As it turned out, I had lots of company. Most of us feel lonely. Emotionally, many of us feel that there is no one around who really can or will understand what we are going through or feeling. This is a lie, of course. But it doesn't feel like a lie. It feels very real.

Upon entering adulthood, I was possessed with the drive to understand my feelings and emotions. I wanted to know why my emotions caused me to *feel* the things I felt, *do* the things I did, *say* the things I said, and *think* the things I thought (many of which seemed to sabotage my pursuits for good, healthy and enjoyable friendships and relationships). The pursuit of this quest led me on a Journey. The Journey turned out to be more of an *emotional* one rather than a physical, psychological or spiritual one. With it, I learned a lot about the human heart, the *emotional*-self.

I discovered that *emotionally*, from the time we are in the womb, we are all without fear, wounding, pain or rejection. From the womb, we feel and perceive love. We feel good about ourselves, our lives and those around us. However, for most of us, somewhere down the road of our lives, wounding invades our hearts.

This invasion occurs at different times for each of us. For some, it occurs when we enter the world. For others, it comes during our early adulthood. Yet, for most of us, it comes in the formative years of our childhood. *Consequently, wounding becomes a part of our formative years: mentally, physically, spiritually and emotionally.* Most of what enters our lives during the formative years seems to become a part of our *behavioral habit patterns.* Thus, the events that cause the wounding, and the feelings spawned by the wounding, stay with us for years. For some, those feelings and memories stay with us to the grave.

I can honestly say I am very happy now. My life has changed radically: *emotionally*, and subsequently physically, spiritually and psychologically. As I mentioned before, the quest to understand my *emotions* and to find my healing led me on a Journey. It was a Journey that allowed me to see *why* my life had changed for the worse as it had done *emotionally*. I learned a lot about many of the "whys" of life while on this Journey. That is what this book is about—some of the "whys" of life.

This understanding is a prerequisite for anyone's emotional healing. You have to understand *why* you "tick" the way you do before you can experience genuine, permanent, long-lasting, *emotional* healing, freedom and peace.

*A Journey to the Other Side of Life* is not about the Journey as a whole. This book is about some of the "whys" of *emotional* life. This book helps you understand why you are the way you are, *emotionally*. It helps you understand why your emotions often control every fiber of your being. This book helps you understand why you *feel* what you feel, *think* what you think, *say* the things you say, and *do* the things you do. This book helps you *shift* your perception.

Several years ago I began offering the experiences of this Journey to others through an organization called The Life Institute in Dallas, Texas. The results and experiences of the many people who have walked through the entire Journey have been phenomenal! This book is being written, not only because of the positive effects that the Journey has had on my life, but also because of the changes so many others have experienced. The Journey is first a *shift in perception*, a change in the way we think and perceive ourselves, life and others. The Journey is also an *emotional process* that leads an individual out of wounding and into emotional love, healing, freedom and peace. The emotional transformation that occurs within the individual is more genuine and permanent than that attained through traditional avenues of emotional healing or self-improvement.

This Journey revolves around fundamentals and principles that differ from those on which most healing and self-improvement perspectives rely. This Journey is *emotionally* focused. It is not physically, psychologically or spiritually focused. This concept is explained later on in the book.

I do not have all of the answers. Nor do I pretend to have all of the answers. Those who know me will quickly agree. But I know the One who does have all of the answers. We can learn a lot about ourselves if we will only stop and listen. This, too, is what this book is about.

I do not pretend to have the qualifications, insight and expertise of a psychologist or psychiatrist. I do not. Nor do I pretend to have all of the qualifications, insights and understandings that a priest, pastor or minister would hold. Though I went through four years of college and four years of graduate school, my qualifications for writing this book and doing what I do through The Life Institute are not born of schooling, degrees, or political or business connections. My qualifications come from a natural, intuitive talent that blends with my own *emotional Journey* through life. This allows me to understand, know and feel what my clients are experiencing, have experienced, and will experience in their lives *emotionally*. This understanding, in turn, gives me (and others who have experienced this Journey) the ability to help others walk through their own emotional Journey—to *shift* their perception and move away from emotional wounding and negative habit patterns and into an emotional life of love, healing, freedom and peace.

I am not espousing a new psychology. I am not promoting a new Gospel. I am not advancing a tenant of New Age. I am simply sharing with you a small part of a very effective process that allows a person to experience  emotional wholeness, love, healing, freedom and peace.

One last thing—as a result of my own experiences through the Journey, I have discovered who I am, how I fit into life's scheme of things, and what I do well. Conversely, I also found that there are many things that I do *not* do well.

We all discover this chilling fact. We copy or parrot others in an attempt to feel the affirming, accepting feelings that accompany the  perceived successes of others. When we fail at their successes, we feel inferior, not affirmed; inadequate, not accepted. This is all the more reason why we each need to find our own emotional healing, who we are and discover what we do well.

I have done that. I have found what I am good at.

I am good at being me. I am *real* good at being me. I like this fact, too. It feels good. No one else is as good at being me as I am. When I am me, I am unique. There is no one quite like me—when I am me.

My mother used to tell me, "You are one in a million, surely God did not make two of you!" Now, I am not so sure this was altogether an affirmation. By my own admission, I was a handful. However, my mother's statement did help entrench within my heart a perceived uniqueness with my life. We all have a uniqueness. But you must discover and unearth your own uniqueness from within. It will not be found outside of you. Your Creator planted it within you. That, too, is what this book is about!

———  ⚓  ———

# Part I

## *Facts About Your Emotional-Self*

*"Above all else, guard your heart,
for it influences everything else in your life."*
**The Bible**

TM

# CHAPTER 1

## *Your Wounded-Self vs. Your Real-Self*
### *Living a Masked Life*

 *H*ave you ever felt as if you were living a lie?

***Scenario 1:*** After a hard day's work, dinner is behind you. You and your mate can finally unwind—together. It is an excellent opportunity to talk about heart issues. But you never do. The risk of opening up to your mate is more than you wish to handle this evening. You reason that the risk involved makes opening up and being real too costly—especially after years of failed attempts. So you live a lie. You refuse to share your inner-most feelings with your mate. But you must share them with some-one, so you call a friend and spend the evening on the phone. Your mate turns on the television and bonds with the characters inside.

***Scenario 2:*** You have always desired to feel a closer connection with your mother or father. But they never seemed to understand you and your feelings in the past. Consequently, you stopped opening up to them years ago. This did not make the problem go away, however. So you still feel empty in your relationship with your parents. You need to share your true feelings with them. You need to feel "connected" with your parents. But the risk of being shunned again is too much. So you live a lie. It is safer. It is also more painful.

***Scenario 3:*** Your best friend is someone you have always felt close to, but you have never fully opened up and shared your deeper feelings with him or her. The thought of doing so is scary. You reason that being that transparent may risk the loss of your friend's acceptance and allegiance. You need the friendship more than you need to be real and honest about your feelings. So you live a lie.

***Scenario 4:*** Over the years, a *self*-concept has developed within you with which you want to disagree. That self-*image* tries to convince you that you are fearful, weak, inadequate or inferior. It has even led you to believe that this is how others see you. To dispel it, you try to project an image of who you wish you were. You know you are not being real, but the risk of facing the fact that you may indeed be inferior or weak is more than you can handle, emotionally. So you live a lie.

In each of the above scenarios you know you are not being real, open, transparent or honest *emotionally* with yourself or with those around you. You know you are projecting a front—an emotional front of strength, happiness, fulfillment or security. You know you are living a lie. You know you are living a masked life. However, you are not alone in this masquerade. Most of us do this all of the time. We do this because of the feelings, fears and emotions we wrestle with day-in and day-out.

The internal feeling can be tormenting at times, can't it? Living a lie often strikes violently against every fiber of your being. It causes you to feel guilt. When left to rule and control your behavior, it can even cause you to feel an element of internal filth. Why? Because living a lie goes against your heart-nature. You and I were created to be real, up front and honest with ourselves, with life and with those around us.

So why do we sometimes live emotional lies? Well, if you are like most of us, you often are not even aware that you are doing these things—living the lies. We often live life oblivious to our feelings and emotions. We are oblivious, that is, until our feelings or emotions *react* to some external stimulus and subsequently take control of our consciousness.

The idea of living life *in touch* with our emotions is foreign to most of us. The thought of doing so can be scary, even paralyzing. The idea of living life with the ability to *channel* and *direct* how our feelings will flow is also foreign to most of us. The idea of being able to *control* our emotions is even more foreign to most of us. Why is this?

Well, to help us better understand why this is often the case, I want to ask you to do an exercise with me. It will not be painful. But it will provoke emotions. What I want you to do is to answer a few questions. Each question relates to your most recent experience with three particular emotions. Please, take your time walking through these questions. I encourage you not to continue reading further until you have sufficiently contemplated each question and your answer to each question. So please relax, take your time and think through this exercise.

*(It may help you to do this exercise by writing your answers on a sheet of paper. If so, take a moment to gather some paper and a pen.)*

**1.** Do you remember the last time you were *angered* or enraged? If you are honest with yourself, it probably wasn't that long ago. How did the anger display itself? What did it cause you to *do*? What did it cause you to *say*? What did it cause you to *think*? What did it cause you to *feel*? Think about it for a moment.

**2.** When was the last time you remember feeling paralyzed with *fear*? How did you respond? What did the fear cause you to *do*? What did it cause you to *say*? What did the fear cause you to *think*? What did it cause you to *feel*? Again, think about it for a moment and record your answers.

**3**. Do you recall the last time you felt down, defeated or even *depressed*? What did the depression cause you to *do*? What did it cause you to *say*? What did it cause you to *think*? What did the depression cause you to *feel*? And again, take just a few moments to think about your answer before moving on.

Chances are you have probably experienced at least one of these emotions (anger, fear or depression) in some form during the past ten days. Most of us have.

What effect does the remembered experiences from the above exercise have on you and your disposition? Does the exercise leave you feeling a little saddened inside, or at a loss for answers? Does it leave you feeling defeated or feeling bad about yourself?

### A Confused Self-Concept

For most of us, the battle with these emotions and others similar to them, often leaves us with intense feelings of confusion, hopelessness or even defeat. Why? Because we feel we have no concrete answers or solutions that will help us conquer our feelings, or bring about genuine healing and change with our emotions.

Consequently, although these emotional experiences are common for you, me and everyone around us, we often try to ignore, deny, and even dismiss these feelings. This is understandable, because they seem to breed so much confusion within our heart and mind.

When we feel and experience these emotions habitually, many of us become convinced that these feelings are a part of, or a reflection of, ourselves and our character. Because of this, the negative wounds, feelings and fears tend to distort and confuse our perception of ourselves. We want to see ourselves as emotionally mature, happy and confident. We want others to see us in a similar light as well. However, when the negative emotions (such as fear, anger and depression) consistently take over our beings and propel such ugliness out of us toward those around us (and toward ourselves), we wind up feeling confused, embarrassed, hurt or ashamed. We fear that these negative fears, feelings and emotions reflect or reveal a dark, ugly or bad side of our inner heart. Consequently, *we become fearful that these negative feelings and their outbursts are reflections of the* real *person inside us.*

At this point our self-concept becomes confusing. We know and want to believe, deep within ourselves, that we are loving, kind and warmhearted individuals. However, this conflicts with the monstrous words, actions or thoughts that thrust themselves out of our minds, mouths and bodies when the negative emotions are rushing us. We feel confused.

We start questioning ourselves:

*"Who am I, really? Am I a kind, caring person, or am I this monster? Which one is the real me?"*

Debilitating, isn't it?

### The Masked Life

In response to the negative feelings and the confusion they breed, a new life takes form. I refer to this new life as *the masked life*. The masked life is our attempt at dispelling feelings and fears of being defective, inferior or bad by projecting an image to ourselves and the outside world of who we wish to be. We want to believe we are loving, kind and warmhearted. We want others to believe we are this way as well. Yet, we are afraid that deep within ourselves, we may be a bad, evil, selfish or inferior person. So, we live and walk in hidden, masked fear as we interact with those around us. We wear the mask to insulate and protect ourselves from the feared idea that we may, in reality, be the monster (the bad, evil, selfish or inferior person) that so often propels itself from our beings.

Many of us live life with the masked fear. It accompanies us everywhere we walk. It goes to bed with us in the evening. It awakens with us in the morning. It hangs over our shoulder throughout the day, whispering to us that we are the very emotional monsters we don't want to be. Is it any wonder we feel confused? That is the power of wounding emotions.

A past client (we will refer to him as Bill) is an example of the masked life. Originally, Bill came to us with his wife. They were seeking help with marriage and relationship problems. As we delved into their situation, we discovered that the greater need lay within the couple's individual emotional healing. They would not be able to heal, restore or build the relationship between the two of them until they each first addressed and changed some individual emotional issues and habit patterns that had plagued each of them for much of their lives.

Bill, because of his emotional wounding, had built a life of entrenched, harsh self-condemnation. His bitterness toward himself was so strong that it was short-circuiting any hopes of him being able to enjoy life or the relationships in his life. In his wounded state, he was incapable of giving love, or receiving love. As we worked through the emotions that affected Bill, we came to the place where he had developed a masked life.

In childhood, Bill had become convinced that he was lazy, selfish and good-for-nothing. His father regularly declared these assessments of Bill during the early, formative years of Bill's childhood. Bill heard these criticisms often. He heard them daily. Emotionally, Bill's internal reaction to this verbal abuse caused him to develop two internal mind-sets. One mind-set reflected the *real* Bill. It was the person that Bill knew was there, a loving, kind and warmhearted person. It was a person who liked life, enjoyed people and felt good about himself. Yet, as Bill's life continued and as the verbal onslaughts continued, Bill began losing touch with his loving, kind and warmhearted self. Bill's *wounded* heart took over when his father's voice was not around. His *wounded* heart spewed voices and feelings that mirrored and affirmed his father's criticisms. These voices and feelings were from Bill's *wounded-self.*

### The Wounded-Self

Bill became accustomed to the voices and feelings of the wounded-self. His wounded-self was the *emotional*-self that had developed as a consequence of the continual verbal abuses. Bill's altered *emotional*-self (his wounded-self) was much more condemning, much less patient, and far less sensitive toward himself and consequently, toward others around him. This disposition, over the years, became a habit lifestyle pattern. It was this habit lifestyle pattern that Bill tried to mask.

This happens with many of us. As the altered emotional lifestyle (the wounded-self) becomes habit, the real battle begins. We try everything to conquer it or disprove it to ourselves (not necessarily to those around us). In spite of this, it usually remains. So we learn to mask it. We learn to cover it up and project what we wish was really there.

Additionally, we begin entertaining the fear that this altered emotional lifestyle may indeed be a reflection of our *real*-self. On one hand we want to believe that, deep within ourselves, we are loving, kind and warmhearted. Yet, on the other hand, we fear that the thoughts, feelings, words and deeds that project themselves from our wounded, altered *emotional*-self are reflections of our *real*-self. So we live the masked life. We live it to numb ourselves from the fear that we may indeed be bad, evil, selfish or inferior.

Over time we feel and become comfortable with the ways of our wounded-self. We live with the wounded-self every day. Many of us lost touch with the feelings of the loving, kind and warmhearted self years earlier. We grow even farther from them over the passing years. Consequently, we feel or fear that these altered, wounded feelings and ways are the truer reflection of our self-nature. At least this is the feeling and fear. To numb ourselves from the pain and fear of this being the truth, we live a masked life with ourselves, as well as with those around us. We try to pretend and convince ourselves and those around us that the negative self-concepts are not valid, all the while feeling and fearing that they are.

*The behavior that spawns from this inner battle is the masked life.* The masked life is one where we say:

"I am not real. I can not be real, with myself, God or others. Why? Because if I am real, I am afraid that the real me will expose itself as the bad, evil, selfish or inferior monster I fear and believe I am."

The fact is, for most of us, we are *not* that monster. Even though we may feel and sound as if we are, we are not. For the most part, we are loving, kind and warmhearted. However, the negative emotions, fears and feelings take over and, through our negative/harmful words and actions, create the effects of a monster protruding from our beings. So, we fear that it reflects the *real*-self. Consequently, we live a masked life.

## The Real-Self (You are loving, kind and warmhearted)

I have learned many things while assisting hundreds of others in their quest for healing and change. One of the lessons learned is that, when unaffected by wounding, and unaffected by the negative influences of others around us, most of us are loving, kind and warmhearted. There are exceptions to this. There are exceptions to any rule. For the most part, however, when left to ourselves (apart from the altered behavior that wounding spawns and apart from any negative external influences of friends, family or other people), most of us do, say, think and produce loving, kind and warmhearted things from within our beings. This happens because the heart from which feelings sprout is, in created form, loving, kind and warmhearted.

It is the wounding that snuffs these good qualities from our beings. It is not because our hearts, in created form, are evil, wicked or monstrous. To conclude this is to conclude that the Creator, who created our hearts, is evil, wicked or monstrous. This just is not so. We, the creation, are created in the "image" of God, the Creator, in His likeness:

*"So God made man like his maker."*
**The Bible**

The reference here is not only to the physical image. It speaks of the mental, spiritual and emotional images as well. Therefore, if our hearts are made in the image of the Creator's heart, then we can be assured that our hearts are loving, kind and warmhearted.

Because of the negative effects and impact that wounding has on our hearts, we produce bad, evil, selfish or wicked thoughts, words, feelings or actions. This is not a reflection of our *real* heart, or *real*-self. It is a reflection of our *wounded* heart, our *wounded*-self.

Some will say, "I can't trust my emotions." This is true of the *wounded*-self. When left to its wounded nature and to the control and influence of other wounded hearts around it, the wounded-self often *does* produce evil, wicked and deceitful things. However, the *real*-self (a whole and healed heart), apart from wounding, and apart from the external influences of other wounded hearts, (a heart the way it was when it was formed in the womb), when left to itself, *will always produce loving, kind and warmhearted fruit.*

Why? How is this so? How is it that by nature, a real, un-wounded heart would produce such good things? Again, it is because the *real*-self is made in the image of the Creator who made it. And we know, by experience and by Biblical principle, that the heart nature of the Creator is good, warm, kind, gentle, loving, compassionate, caring, forgiving and patient:

*"...for God is love."*
*"...for He is full of tenderness and mercy."*
**The Bible**

Therefore, the *real* you, your *real*-self—your inward heart or *emotional*-self—is a *mirrored reflection* of the heart of your Creator. The wounded you is a reflection of the wounded, fearful heart of humanity.

### Understanding Your *Emotional*-Self

Well, if the idea that we are loving, kind and warmhearted is true, how can you and I get a handle on the wounded, negative emotions and the behaviors they create? The first step is to gain an appropriate understanding of yourself and who you are *emotionally*, your *emotional*-self.

Understanding your *emotional*-self will allow you to know and understand:

⇨ why relationships have been a revolving door in your life; or

⇨ why you have had difficulty holding a steady, fulfilling job; or

⇨ why your feelings would cause you to verbally or physically strike out at those closest to you.

Gaining a clear understanding of your *emotional*-self will help you understand why you battle with anger, fear, depression or any other negative, defeating emotion.

A clear understanding of your *emotional*-self will help you know what you need to do to conquer anger, fear, depression or any other detrimental emotion. This understanding will also put you on the path toward controlling your feelings and emotions.

So, how can you experience genuine and permanent emotional healing, and also change your mental, emotional, physical and verbal behavior?

1. By acquiring an *understanding* of yourself *emotionally*, and how your *emotional*-self functions and influences your mental, emotional, physical and verbal behavior.

2. This understanding comes by discovering how wounding works; how it affects you and your entire being, mentally, emotionally, spiritually and physically.

We will attempt to accomplish the first objective through this section ("Part I: Facts About Your *Emotional*-Self") of

*A Journey to the Other Side of Life.* With this in mind, there are five distinct concepts we will  discuss in the next five chapters:

1. Who you are (Chapter Two),
2. How wounding affects your mental, emotional, physical and verbal behavior (Chapter Three)
3. Where emotional pain comes from (Chapter Four),
4. Why past attempts at emotional healing, happiness and change have failed (Chapter Five), and
5. What effects you can have on your thoughts, feelings and disposition (Chapter Six).

In "Part II: The Wounded-Self," we will accomplish our second objective. We will discover just how wounding works. We will walk through the metamorphic behavioral transformation and change that occurs within you and me when wounding and pain enters our *emotional*-self.

In the last section of *A Journey to the Other Side of Life* ("Part III: The Other Side of Life: Your Real-Self"), we will explore in depth, your *emotional*-self as a whole, healed, free and complete entity within you. We will look at the way your *emotional*-self was created and intended to be, before wounding "rooted" in and began it's life-altering, life-changing process within your life.

———————⚓———————

*Remember & Reflect*

1. *Because of wounding and the fear that our **real**-self may be bad, evil, defective, inferior or wicked, many of us adopt a masked life approach to living.*
2. *When unaffected by wounding and unaffected by the negative influences of others around us, most of us are loving, kind and warmhearted. We are good people, with tender, caring hearts.*
3. *In order to experience emotional healing and change, you first must get to know and understand your **emotional**-self.*

# CHAPTER 2

# *Who Are You?*
## *An Entity Consisting of Four Parts*

*"The heart of him that has understanding seeks knowledge."*
*"Those things which proceed out of the mouth come from the heart."*
**The Bible**

$\mathscr{H}$elen came to us con-
fused and perplexed. She was not one who was plagued by some
major, traumatic wounding or event from her past or present life.
She was just very confused about the relationships in her life.

Previously divorced after twelve years of marriage, Helen
was engaged to marry again. Outwardly, she gave all of the signs
of excitement and anticipation for her upcoming wedding. Her
first marriage had been an emotional wasteland. Though there
never had been any obvious external negative events (such as
physical, sexual or verbal abuse, rejection or abandonment) within
the first marriage, it had been an emotional desert—a wasteland.
There had been no heart-to-heart communication or relationship
during the entirety of the marriage.

This new relationship was a stark contrast to the first. The
groom-to-be was emotionally and verbally open, transparent and
stimulating. He was alive—emotionally! He interacted with

Helen verbally and physically. The feeling that this companion-ship gave Helen was indescribable. It seemed to be everything she had ever hoped for.

So why was Helen coming to us? What was there to be con-fused or perplexed about?

Helen came to us because she was having difficulty entering into a marriage relationship with the fiance. It wasn't anything in particular about the fiance. As we mentioned already, he was wonderful. For some unknown reason, Helen could not proceed with the marriage, and she could not understand why.

Each time she would take a closer step toward this new rela-tionship, Helen found her heart (her emotions) wanting to step back. Initially, this constant internal struggle confused Helen. By the time we saw her, she was more than confused. She had moved in and out of a confirmed commitment to marry several times. After months of living with her internal emotional roller coaster, Helen had begun to doubt her own stability, mentally and emotionally.

It was easy to see why Helen had developed her doubts. In an attempt to resolve her feelings and find the solutions, Helen had tried psychological therapy. This only left her doubting her sanity and mental stability. Helen also tried to get her answers spiritually. She began to conclude that all of her mixed feelings, which by this time were causing some very extreme negative behaviors, were a sign from God that she was possibly deep in sin and therefore distant from her Creator. This reasoning only brought further confusion and fear. The fear eventually para-lyzed Helen—mentally, emotionally and physically. Helen grew to the point where, because of the confusion and fear, she was incapable of making a decision, any decision, and moving for-ward with it.

Why was this so? How had Helen gotten to this extreme point? Helen did not understand that her existence consisted of four distinct parts, with one of those parts being her *emotional-self*. All of her life, Helen had either grouped her feelings in with her mind or had tried to dismiss them altogether. Finally, Helen's inability to function and make basic decisions caused her to deal with this dilemma. After Helen learned that her hesitancy was coming from her heart, or *emotional*-self, she then was able to probe her feelings and uncover her apprehensions about her upcoming marriage. As things turned out, Helen discovered that she was unable to pursue her second marriage because she still held a deeply seeded *emotional* hope that her first marriage would somehow change for the better, *emotionally*. There had been a hidden desire within Helen that the first relationship would be the emotionally rewarding and fulfilling relationship she had always wanted it to be (even though by now her husband, who had left Helen, was already remarried). Holding on to that emotional hope kept Helen's heart from being able to move forward in any new emotional commitment.

With this discovery, we walked Helen through a process that allowed her to let go of the emotions and hopes she had not resolved. Once this had occurred within her, Helen was then able to move forward with her life. In short, we helped Helen to discover who she was.

Who are you and who am I? Emotional wounding and pain often leave many of us feeling confused about who we are. Why? Because we do not understand why we *feel* some of the things we feel, or *do* some of the things we do, or *say* some of the things we say, or *think* some of the things we think. Consequently, we have difficulty understanding who we are and how we feel.

When there is a lack of understanding, we naturally conclude CONFUSION. We approach everything this way. If our automobile breaks down, what do we do? How do we react? What do we say to ourselves?

*"It's too confusing for me. I'll call the repairman."*

We live in a society of "specialists." Why? Because this has become the easiest way for us to deal with our own confusion or misunderstanding regarding many areas of our lives. Consequently, we have become accustomed to retaining quick answers and quick solutions. The only problem in using this approach with our emotions is that there are no quick solutions for matters involving our *emotional*-self. There are answers and solutions, but none are quick.

### A Lack of Understanding Produces Confusion

Using the illustration of a tree: if we try to produce answers, or a change of fruit, by focusing exclusively on the fruit, our efforts will not be very productive. Why? Because we must focus our efforts and energy on the *root*—not the fruit—if we want to experience good, positive change in the fruit (see Illus. 2–1). This sounds logical, doesn't it? So our attention and energy needs to be focused on the root—a lack of understanding of self (especially the *emotional*-self)—not on the fruit or the produced feelings of confusion.

Illus. 2–1: **A Lack of Understanding Produces Confusion.**

The lack of an understanding of our feelings and *emotional-self* is at the root, or foundation, of our difficulty with healing and change. This root produces subsequent feelings of confusion.

The confused feelings surface when we find ourselves realizing things like:

*"Why did I react with those words when my mate said what he or she said?"*

or

*"Why did I react with that physical action when my child broke my valued possession?"*

By nature, you and I *react* to the feelings of confusion. These feelings consume our attention. Consequently, our focus is *distracted* away from the root issue—a lack of understanding—which, when dealt with, holds the key to our needed remedy and solution.

### We Consist of Four Parts, or Realms

Are we complex complicated human entities? No. The starting point for understanding ourselves and our emotions is to first realize that we each, by design, consists of four distinct parts, or realms of life and experience:

a body,
a spirit,
a mind/will, and
an *emotional*-self.

Technically speaking, it is more accurate to say that we consist of three parts: a body, a spirit, and a soul (with the soul consisting of the mind, will and emotions). However, in dealing with and working on the *emotional*-self within a person, we have found our efforts to be much more productive if we are able to help the client conceptualize the *emotional*-self as a completely separate entity from the other aspects of his or her being. If you and I were graphically separated into these four parts or realms, we might look something like Illus. 2–2 below.

Let's take a moment to look at each of these four parts.

## The Four Parts of Man/Woman

**body**    **spirit**    **mind/will**    *emotional*-**self**

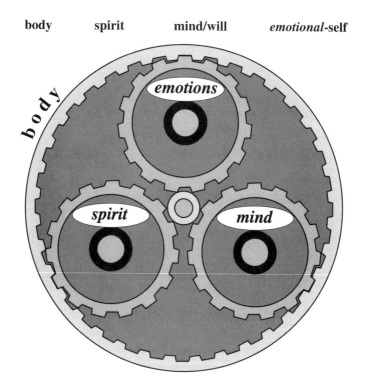

**\*All are distinctly separate in *form*, but interdependent and interrelated in *function*.**

Illus. 2–2: **The Four Parts of a Man & Woman**

### Your Body

Your body is a *shell*. It is your carcass. It is the physical, fleshly instrument that holds and contains all of you and who you are, while you are on this earth, in this lifetime.

### Your Spirit

Your spirit is the part of you that allows you to *know* and *perceive* the existence of your Creator. Notice I didn't say "believe in" your Creator. That really is not the issue here.

Whether we believe in our Creator has nothing to do with *knowing* and *perceiving* the existence of our Creator. Often, when we are severely hurt and wounded emotionally, we may have unresolved negative or painful fears, feelings and emotions. We sometimes place the blame for our negative emotions, and the events that triggered them, upon our Creator. This, in turn, sets in motion additional unresolved, conflicting inner feelings toward the One who made us. At some point, it becomes easier to mentally, emotionally, physically and verbally convince ourselves of the nonexistence of a Creator than to ferret through many conflicting and confusing hurts, wounds and emotions.

However, regardless of these conclusions, spiritually, deep inside the human creation there is an inner sense of the presence and reality of the Creator.

### Your Mind/Will

This is your psychological being. It is your intellect, your mind. It is the part of you that has the capacity to make willful choices.

What do I mean by "willful choices"? All of us make choices constantly. We make choices from one of two realms within ourselves:

1. from our minds, as decisions of the will; or
2. from our *emotional*-self, based on what we are feeling or fearing.

Without realizing it, many of us make choices and decisions with regard to our lives based on wounded feelings, fears and emotions, not based on willful decisions that come from our character and heart-nature. However, we would never admit to this. To do so would be a sign of weakness and a source of confusion.

Yet, it is a fact. *We make most of our decisions, not based on who we are in our hearts through willful choices, but based on what we are feeling or fearing at any given moment.*

When wounding, fear or painful feelings cause our powerful *emotional*-self to rage out of control, many of us attempt to use our minds to circumvent or corral these emotions. This then forces our mind to perform a role it was not intended to perform—that of watchdog or lord over our emotions and life. In addition to this, while our minds convince and deceive us into believing that everything is under control, our wounded fears, feelings and emotions are dictating and controlling our spiritual, mental, physical and emotional behavior. Consequently, our ploy to use our minds to produce emotional peace always ends in failure. Ultimately, this action only produces *more* confusion, hopelessness and defeat emotionally, as well as mentally and relationally.

Ideally, in a world full of love, peace and joy, separated from fear and wounding, the mind is to serve as a *channel* through which the *emotional*-self (free from fear, free from wounding, full of love) can freely express itself toward the human entity it lives within and toward others in life. However, that would only work in an ideal world, a world without fear and wounding.

But this is the real world, right? Well, it is possible to live, function and exist within such a world. It happens when we refuse to allow ourselves to be *victims* of the world around us. It happens when we *take control* (mentally, physically and emotionally) of our personal world, our lives, relationships and activities.

### Your *Emotional*-Self

Your *emotional*-self is the core, or center, of your life. It is that part of you that allows you to experience life and express your uniqueness into life around you. The Bible often refers to your *emotional*-self as your *"heart"*. Discovering how the Bible refers to the heart is a rewarding and enlightening experience. Through such research, it becomes obvious that Someone, somewhere, places a whole lot of emphasis on the heart, or the *emotional*-self of the human entity.

The heart, or *emotional*-self , is intended to be a major, powerful and positive force within our lives. The things that are intended to spring from it (peace, love and joy to name just a few) are what give you and me our zeal, drive and motivation for living and enjoying this experience we refer to as "life".

Many of us are trained from infancy to perceive life through a physical perspective. As we progress into our school age years, we learn to perceive life through a mental, psychological or intellectual perspective. As we continue to mature into the world around us, we also learn to conceptualize life through a spiritual perspective. Yet, for most of us, no one ever teaches us or tells us *how* to perceive life from an *emotional* perspective. This idea is totally foreign to most of us. It doesn't make sense. Why? Because we have never done it before. In all of my years of introducing clients to the emotionally-focused perspective of living, I have not crossed paths with one individual who perceived life and life's experiences through the emotional realm of life. Interesting, isn't it?

Most of us are so accustomed to perceiving and functioning only through a spiritual, physical or intellectual perspective that the thought of perceiving and conceptualizing life through the emotional realm is very disconcerting. By habit, we perceive and receive life through the physical, mental or spiritual perspective before considering the emotional perspective.

Genuine, fulfilling relationships (whether physical/human or spiritual relationships) are experienced through the *emotional* realm, not the mental or physical realms of life. Think about it. Have you ever had a good, rewarding, stimulating relationship with anyone through the realm of your mind or intellect? Rarely, if ever! It sounds rather boring, doesn't it? The reason for this is simple. Our Creator intended for us to be *emotional* creatures *first*, not physical or mental ones (remember the heart, or *emotional*-self, is at the core or center of life). Consequently, any fulfilling or rewarding relationship, communication or conversation that we have with others is always because it is a *heart-based* encounter. Fulfilling and successful relationships and communication are always *heart*-based, *not* head-based.

Heart-based relationships and communication stimulate your *heart*, or *emotional*-self. This, in turn, motivates you to have an interest in, or even further pursue, the relationship or conversation. This makes very good sense, doesn't it? Yet, some who attempt to perceive and live life solely through the realm of their intellect have a very dry and unstimulating life. Don't take my word for it, though; just ask their children, friends, or spouse. Without fail, the recipients of a head-based relationship will attest to its morbidity.

How can you distinguish the differences between the mental and emotional aspects of your life? A simple way of doing this is to remember that the mental realm deals with what you are *thinking* and the emotional realm pertains to what you are *feeling*. This is rather important, so let's look at it again:

*"My mental-self reflects what I am* thinking.
*My emotional-self reflects what I am* feeling.*"

Both produce two completely different effects within your consciousness. Yet, because of a lack of understanding—misunderstanding—we tend to lump the two realms into one. Doing this results in feelings and thoughts of confusion.

During the duration of our counseling service's emotional healing and life-improvement process with an individual, we focus as much as *ninety percent* of our energies on a client's *emotional*-self. The remaining ten percent is directed toward the client's mind and will. For the most part, we do not focus our attention on the spiritual or physical realms. The client usually does, however. This is because when the *emotional*-self is out of balance, the imbalance filters over into the other three areas of an individual's life. Consequently, there is a natural desire to bring his or her entire being (mental, emotional, physical and spiritual) into balance.

We will approach the remainder of this book in a similar manner. Our focus will be on the *emotional*-self. Consequently, I will be relating with you from an *emotional* perspective, *not* physical, mental (psychological or intellectual) or spiritual. As we walk through the principles of your feelings and heart, try to remember this with me. Try to perceive what you are reading from an *emotional perspective*. If you can do this I think you will be very pleased with the experience and results.

————— ❧ —————

*Remember & Reflect*  **1.** *A lack of understanding with regard to our emotions and our **emotional**-self, produces confusion.*

**2.** *By nature, we focus our attention on the feelings and thoughts of confusion (the fruit) and thereby react to them, rather than trying to understand where they come from (the root).*

*3. By design, your human entity consists of four distinct parts or realms:*

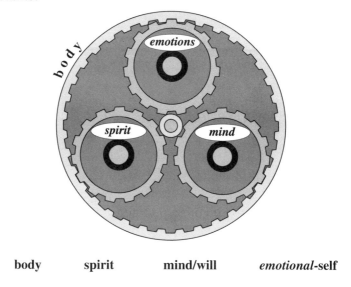

**body          spirit          mind/will          *emotional*-self**

**\*All are distinctly separate in *form*, but interdependent and interrelated in *function*.**

*4. It is important that we learn to perceive life from an **emotional** perspective rather than a physical, mental (intellectual) or spiritual perspective. We will approach the remainder of our discussions in this book from the **emotional** perspective. So, try to perceive life through your **emotional**-self during the next few days.*

# CHAPTER 3

# *How Wounding Works*
## *The Anatomy of a Wart*

$\mathcal{I}$ hate warts, don't you? Do you know of anyone who likes warts? If you do, I am sure you keep a measured distance between yourself and that person, don't you? Have you ever had a wart? Many of us have. Most of us are familiar with the little brown warts that our peers convinced us came from frogs. You know the type of wart I am speaking about. Its color is darker than your skin and it grows as a round lump on the surface of your skin. Most of us are very familiar with this kind of wart. However, this isn't the type of wart we are referring to here.

At this point you may be thinking, *"Why are we talking about warts? What do warts have to do with my feelings and emotions?"*

It does seem off the wall from our topic at hand, doesn't it? It is not, though. Here is why. Emotions such as fear, anger and depression are merely symptoms. They are not all inclusive, in

43

and of themselves. That is, these emotions and others like them are outward fruits, manifestations or symptoms of more deeply rooted, inward causes. In other words, emotions such as fear, anger and depression are results of deeper, internal wounds that have come into your heart, mind and life at some point in your past. Those deep, internal wounds went through a type of metamorphosis and ultimately manifested themselves externally through such emotions as fear, anger or depression.

To better understand how this emotional process works within the heart, we will study the process and effect that a wart has on you and me when it attaches itself to the skin. More specifically, we will look at a plantar wart. Have you ever heard of a plantar wart? Its similarity with the emotional process that is affected by wounding within the human heart is remarkable.

### The Invasion of a Plantar Wart

A plantar wart attaches itself to the outer surfaces of your skin. On the surface it looks and feels as if it is a part of your skin. In fact, during the early days of its growth, you are not even aware of the wart's existence. However, within a matter of weeks, once its size allows for greater strength, you become very aware of the plantar wart's presence. Once big enough, the plantar wart has the look and feel of a corn on your skin. It is hard and crusty to the touch, but it looks as if it is a part of your skin. It's color, or pigment, is the same as that of your skin. It adapts to fit you, it's environment. It's not a darker shade, like the intruder mentioned in the first paragraph.

On the surface, the wart looks as if it is a part *of* you and your skin. In reality though, the plantar wart is an *invader*. It is an invader that has attached itself *to* your skin (see Illus. 3–1). Once firmly in place, the plantar wart sends its roots, like tentacles, through your skin and into your body. Its life source is your blood. As the plantar wart grows, it begins to act as if it owns your body. It takes over, literally. Anytime something or someone comes along and brushes up against the wart's outer surface,

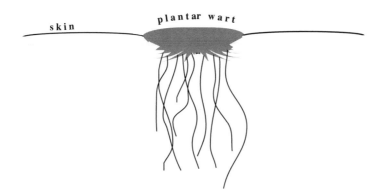

Illus. 3–1: **Anatomy of a Plantar Wart**

it shoots  sharp pain through its roots into your body. Your body reacts accordingly.

After this happens repeatedly, you become consumed with the presence of the plantar wart and its power over your body and mind.  It begins to direct your every thought and decision. Repeated often enough, these *reactions* to the wart become *habit*. Before you know it, you have developed habits based on some wart that has attached itself to your flesh. The wart triggers pain. You react to the pain. Eventually, your reactions become habits. *An invader has altered your behavior.*

A wart triggers *pain*;
     you *react* to the pain;
          when repeated often enough,
               your reactions become *habits.*

### The Invasion of Emotional wounding

Emotional wounding works in a similar fashion.  It enters your heart through the avenues of your *mind* and *body*.  Your mind and body are the *channels* through which the wounding travels before it arrives at its destination—your heart, or *emotional*-self. Emotional wounding can enter your life wearing many different suits.  The wounding may enter your heart in the form of a divorce—either your own divorce or the divorce of your parents or someone else extremely close to you emotionally. It may also enter your heart through the death or loss of someone to whom you were emotionally close. Wounding may invade your heart through incest or sexual abuse, as a child or as an adult. It may violate you through the intense and regular physical, verbal or even nonverbal abuse you received either as a child or as an adult. Wounding may enter your heart through the loss of a job or the breakup of a close relationship. The list could go on and on. What is important to understand at this point is that the *emotional wounding enters your heart, mind and life through some form of violation, wrong or encroachment placed upon you, uninvited.* It enters and travels through the avenues of your mind and body in order to arrive at its destination: your heart (see Illus. 3–2).

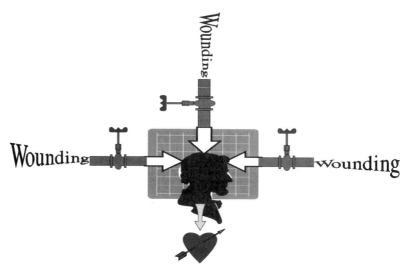

Illus. 3–2: **Wounding Entering Through the Mind and Body.**

Now, let's follow the path that both the wart and the emotional wounding take and you will see how wounding works: how it affects your life and alters your behavior, mentally, verbally, physically and emotionally.

### The Wound is the Real Enemy

*External invaders (wounding), can and do alter your mental, emotional, physical and verbal behavior.* Just like the plantar wart, the emotional wounding invades your life. It attaches itself to your heart in the same way that the wart attaches itself to your skin. It is important to understand that the wounding attaches itself *to* you—to your *emotional*-self. It is *not* a part *of* you. To say that the wound, and all the thoughts and feelings it has spawned, are a part of you would be like saying the wart is a part of you. No! It is not a part of you. Like the plantar wart, the emotional wounding may *feel* as if it is a part of you. But it is not. It is attached *to* you. Do you see the distinction? This is important, because after years of living with the pain and reality of the wound, you become convinced that it *is* a part of you—that it is a reflection of who you are. It is not. It is a reflection of the *wounded* you. It is *not* a reflection of the *real* you, the person you were created to be while in the womb.

After the invasion or attachment, the wound, like the wart, takes up residence within your heart. In addition to this, just like the wart, anytime someone says something or does something in such a way as to touch, trigger or press against that old wounding (just like pressing up against the outer surface of the wart), it thrusts waves of emotional pain and memory through your being.

Immediately, you *react* to the pain that the wounding has caused. You are not reacting to the person or event that has touched off or *triggered* the painful emotion. You are reacting to the pain. However, your mind's eye rivets its attention on the external trigger—the person or event that triggered the pain. Your mind convinces you that the external trigger is the source of your pain and discomfort. But it is not. The wounding is the real culprit. The wound, like the wart, is your real enemy.

However, in the midst of negative wounding, pain and emotion, we can not see the true enemy. We become convinced that our real enemy and source of pain is the external trigger—the person who did or said something, or the outward event which took place, that triggered our pain. We focus our blame on the external trigger  rather than the wounded feelings or fears because it is easier to perceive through one of our five senses (hearing, seeing, feeling, touching or tasting). We can't hear, feel, see, touch or taste the internal emotional wounding. It isn't a physical object. But we can readily hear, feel, see, touch and taste the external trigger. The person or event triggering our fears or feelings *is* tangible and concrete. So we focus our blame on what we can understand and grasp through our physical senses—such as the mate who triggers feelings of emotional abandonment, or the job which triggers a feeling of inferiority.

It is very difficult to try to conceptualize the wounding inside us. In Chapter Two we learned that our reactions to wounding and pain often produce feelings of confusion. We react to the confusion with blame. Instead, we need to focus our energies on understanding our *emotional*-self (the root), not on the confusing feelings and fears (the fruit).

### Remember from Chapter Two

Instead of trying to acquire an understanding into the "root" of the problem or negative emotion, many of us, by nature, will focus our attention on the outward thoughts and feelings of confusion.

> ➥ Consequently, we *react* to the feelings of confusion, rather than trying to understand our emotions and their source.

>> ➥ Our reaction to the confusion ultimately breeds *more* confusion. This, in turn, leads to feelings of hopelessness, defeat or depression.

It is important to realize that the external triggers in your life are not the sources of your emotional pain. The external people and events are only *triggers*. The source of the pain is the wounding, encroachment or violation that happened to you in the past. *The wounding is what has altered your behavior.* The people and events in your everyday life only serve to *trigger* what was already in existence emotionally, no matter how long the wound has been dormant before being triggered. Blaming the triggers would be like blaming the external things and people who brush up against you when the plantar wart shoots its pain through your body.

Most of us stay blinded to this fact. We live our lives trying, in vain, to remove or cut off all of the triggers that trigger our emotional pain. However, this is fruitless. In the process of doing this we destroy some very good, meaningful and healthy relationships and business opportunities along the path of our lives. We move from relationship to relationship and from job to job. We keep burning bridges, convincing ourselves that the next relationship, or the next job, will be better. Often, it is not. Within twelve to eighteen months, the changed environment has not produced freedom from the emotional pain. Why? Because triggers are everywhere. They always will be. The triggers are not the problem. The wounding inside you and me, and more specifically, how the wounding affects you and me, is at the core of the problem. It is important that we understand this fact. This is why a change of relationships, jobs or residence doesn't necessarily ensure a peace of mind or life. How you and I *react* to the external triggers in our lives—the relationships, jobs and events around us—determines our level of emotional peace, freedom and happiness.

When you pursue a change as a flight from emotional pain, it rarely works. It only works when the change occurs because the old environment doesn't fit your whole and healed heart nature anymore. Now remember, there is a big difference between your heart nature and your wounded nature. You are born with your heart nature. You acquire your wounded nature as a consequence of emotional wounding. Those who are absorbed in the latter usually have lost touch with the former.

### How Wounding Alters Our Behavior
*How you **react** to the external triggers in your life (the relationships, jobs and events around you) determines your level of emotional love, freedom, peace and happiness.*

So, how has wounding from the past altered your mental, verbal, physical and emotional behavior? Again, to understand how this happens, let's look at the wart.

As the wart grows, it roots its tentacles through your skin, into your body. As it enlarges, the pain it injects also increases. Along with this, it is touched or pressed regularly over time, by external triggers. This contact thrusts pain through your body. By instinct, you react to the pain. When this scenario occurs over and over, repeatedly, your *reactions* to the pain become *habit*.

Emotional wounding works identically to this. When the external triggers in your life trigger the feelings, pain and memories of the past, you *react* to that pain. When your reactions are repeated time after time, your reactions become *habit*. The habits that are created can be mental habits (attitudes and thoughts), emotional habits (feelings and fears), physical habits (outward and physical acts or actions), and verbal habits (words and phrases).

These habits, when repeated often enough, alter and even take over your behavior. Before you know it, you are doing, saying, thinking and feeling things that do not reflect who you believe yourself to be in your heart. They do not reflect who you actually are, either. But since they are constantly coming from your being, you conclude that they are a reflection of the real you. This then triggers an inner battle within you:

*You know these things are not a part of the real you. Yet, they look, sound and feel as if they are a part of the real you. So, you feel confused. You become terrified and afraid that these things may be a reflection of the real you. Consequently, you take on the masked approach to life* (as in Chapter One).

Emotional wounding triggers *pain*;
      you *react* to the pain;
            when repeated often enough,
                  your reactions become *habits*.

However, it is important to remember that these outward re-actions to emotional wounding and pain are *not* a reflection of the *real* you. They are a reflection of the *wounded* you. Those negative and detrimental thoughts, feelings, words and actions are the result of something that has *attached* itself *to* you (emo-tional wounding) like a wart attaches itself to your body. The negative thoughts, feelings, words and actions are *not* a part of the *real* you. They may feel as if they are, in the same way that the wart gives you the impression and feeling that *it* is a part of the real you. They are not though. This is very important, so let's look at it again:

*All of the negative thoughts, feelings, words and actions that come out of you are not a reflection of the **real** you. They are a reflection of the **wounded** you.*

Now, at first sight, this may seem to be a very irresponsible perspective. It can be, but it is not. On the contrary, when you accept this perspective, you are taking responsibility for who you are and how you feel. You refuse to blame others for your prob-lems and pain. At this point you are able to move toward genu-ine love, healing, freedom and peace and away from the wounds and their effects on your life. The opposite approach, that of blaming the external triggers in your life for the pain you experi-ence, is by far a much more irresponsible perspective in life. It causes you to live a life of blame. You end up blaming and hold-ing other people responsible for *who you are*, *how you feel,* and *the circumstances surrounding your life*. This irresponsible per-spective is fruitless and often leads a person into depression and depressive behavior. We will explore this perspective in greater detail in Part II. Before doing that, however, let's explore where our emotional pain comes from. What are the "roots" of emo-tional wounding? We will discover these roots in Chapter Four.

*Remember & Reflect*   *1. As with the plantar wart, **external** feelings, fears and emotions are **triggered** by deeply rooted **internal** emotional wounding.*

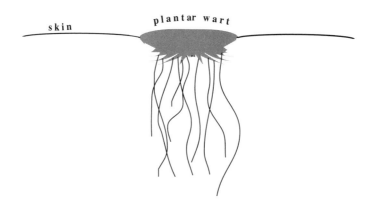

skin     plantar wart

2. *External invaders (wounding) can and do **alter** your mental, emotional, physical and verbal behavior.*

3. *How you **react** to the externals in your life (the relationships, jobs and events around you) determines your level of emotional love, freedom, peace and happiness.*

4. *Emotional wounding triggers pain;*
     *you **react** to the pain;*
          *when repeated often enough,*
               *your reactions become* habits.

5. *These habits are directly determined by how you **react** to the wounding, inwardly within yourself, and outwardly toward those around you.*

6. *All of the negative thoughts, feelings, words and actions that come out of you are **not** a reflection of the **real** you. They are a reflection of the **wounded** you.*

# CHAPTER 4

# *Three Sources of Emotional Pain*
## *Where Wounding Comes From*

*W*hy is it that our best attempts at emotional healing, happiness or change are often met with failure? We try psychotherapy, but the pain remains. We can cope with our problems better, but the pain remains. We try spiritual counseling or ministry. This seems to work for a while, but often, the old patterns and pain return. We try lectures, books and tapes in an attempt to *intellectually* grasp an *emotional* function. However, the problem remains. We try new relationships or new jobs. Yet, the good emotions and changes that come with "a fresh start," or a changed environment, are often only temporary. The old feelings and fears soon resurface. Failed attempts at finding genuine and permanent emotional healing or behavioral change is a dilemma experienced often by many of us.

In order to effectively and genuinely deal with the emotional pain and the patterns of behavior they create, we need a clear understanding of the pain's source or "root."

This fact was never more evident to us than when we began meeting with Ben. Ben came to us because of past failed attempts at conquering anger, rejection, performance-based living and perfectionism. Prior to coming to us, Ben spent years trying to conquer these emotional mountains in his life. He went through all of the traditional channels—psychological therapy, spiritual counseling, books, tapes—everything he could think of, all to no avail. By the time we met Ben, he was more knowledgeable with the professional language for his problems than are most trained professionals.

Ben had been raised in what most of us would consider the ideal, all-American home. His father had a good paying professional job. His mother worked at home as a housewife and mother. Ben and his siblings were the recipients of a very comfortable home life. He had not experienced any major, traumatic wounding or obvious, negative events in his life.

As we began walking Ben through our process, we encountered the root of his wounding. Ben's father was never around while Ben was growing up. He was an absentee father, emotionally and physically. He worked all day and did his own thing in his off hours. For Ben's father, "his own thing" meant things like: golf at the country club regularly, and watching football, baseball, basketball or some other sporting event on the television with his buddies.

Because of his father's life style, Ben grew up feeling intense feelings of rejection and abandonment. These feelings produced emotional behavioral patterns of rejection and performance-based living. He also grew up with an insatiable inner feeling that he never measured up to the acceptance of anyone around him. Consequently, Ben developed a life style of trying to disprove and dispel (inwardly and externally to others around him) these feelings and fears. He relied on perfectionism and performance-based living in an attempt to squelch his wounded feelings and fears. However, all of this only served to produce an intense dissatisfaction within Ben which he felt toward himself, his life and others.

Our first objective in our sessions with Ben was to identify Ben's wounding, and walk him through a process of emotional healing. Upon doing this however, Ben's old behavior remained. The changes we were expecting were not surfacing. So we continued forward.

Our next procedure involved walking Ben through an exercise we refer to as the Iron Claws Process. In short, we helped Ben uncover and gain freedom from many painful, unfulfilled emotional expectations he had carried throughout much of his life. The baggage of his unfulfilled emotional expectations was more than many of us have to deal with in a lifetime. When you add the pain from these unfulfilled emotional expectations to the hurt that resulted from the wounding, the burden and weight can be tremendous. It was for Ben.

So we walked Ben through this second exercise of healing and freedom from the hurt and pain of past unfulfilled emotional expectations. However, his old behavioral patterns still remained. Ben had several bad habits that were not going away and they continued to produce more pain and wounding within Ben. They seemed unconquerable. Those habits were:

1. An extremely vulgar vernacular, partly as a release mechanism for his anger and temper, and partly as an attempt to feel accepted by his peers.

2. Regular battles with intense feelings of not fitting in, not belonging and feeling rejected.

3. A negative, critical attitude and perspective toward himself, life and others. Ben tended to see everything and everyone in a negative light.

At this point you may be wondering, *"What was going on with this guy? Why wasn't he changing?"* Many would wonder this. However, Ben did change. But only after we walked him through a third process which replaced the old, destructive behavioral *habits* which had been formed in *reaction* to his past hurt and wounding, with new, positive habits. We specifically addressed each negative habit one at a time. Ben's old behavioral habits were conquered and replaced by new, more pleasurable, mental, emotional, physical and verbal behavioral habits.

The point of Ben's story is that it was not enough for Ben to experience healing from his past emotional wounding alone. Nor was it enough for Ben to feel freedom from the pain of his unfulfilled emotional expectations. Ben also had to be freed from many negative and detrimental behavioral habits that had developed over the years in reaction to his hurt and pain.

Ben's battle with wounding is very typical. From his story we can learn a major truth:

> *There are three sources or "roots" of emotional pain:*
>     *wounding,*
>     *unfulfilled emotional expectations,* and
>     *habits,* spawned by wounding and unfulfilled
>         expectations.

### Wounding
Many of us are all too familiar with this one.

You hurt because someone, somewhere down the road of your life, *hurt* you, *violated* you, *betrayed* you, or *wounded* you. The pain and wounding may have entered your life as a one-time event, or as a series of occurrences. The only thing you know for certain is that the pain has been with you for a long time.

There is a plethora of books on the market today addressing this one source of emotional pain. It seems that everyone now has the answer and cure for our emotional ailments. Their solutions most often center around the wounding in our lives. So why is it that we can go through a very legitimate process of emotional healing of past wounds and still have the old patterns and pain consistently resurface and plague us?

Usually, it is because there are *two* additional sources of emotional pain, and neither has yet been reckoned with. It is not enough to deal only with the emotional wounds of the heart. In order to effectively conquer and control emotional pain, and the resulting bad habits, we must also deal with the remaining sources of our emotional conflicts:  unfulfilled emotional expectations and habits.

### Unfulfilled emotional expectations

Have you ever felt *hurt, let down, frustrated* or *disappointed*? Sure you have. But, has it ever hit you so hard that you thought you would die if you had to feel this much pain for the rest of your life? Draining, wasn't it? Well, chances are you were not experiencing this pain because of wounding. In all likelihood, you experienced this pain within your heart because of some *unfulfilled emotional expectation* you had placed on someone or something around you.

Subconsciously, you were looking to a person, activity or job to perform or work out in a certain way. But it did not happen as you had hoped or expected. The resulting disappointment was more than you had bargained for, emotionally.

Instinctively, you and I have a tendency to blame the person or event on whom we place our hope or expectation, for the resulting pain we experience when our hope or expectation is shattered. However, they are not to blame. We are to blame. We set ourselves up for the pain when we place our hopes, demands or expectations on the people or things around us.

Often, out of a pure and innocent desire to feel unconditional love, acceptance, value or worth, we will subconsciously place unspoken, emotional hopes, desires, demands or expectations on others. We usually place these expectations on those closest to us. When we do, the dynamics of the relationship change. Unconditional acceptance and freedom are lost. The relationship then takes a turn for the worse. Often the other person feels the pressure of our expectations. It feels very oppressive, restrictive and confining causing that person to pull away. This pulling away creates a feeling of rejection within us, which is the last thing we need to experience.

Without being aware of it, many of us have a lot of emotional pain and fear. In addition to that, we also have a lot of destructive habit patterns webbed within our lives because of the pain from unfulfilled emotional expectations which we have placed on the things and people around us.

So, to experience genuine and permanent emotional relief, healing and change, we each must experience healing, not only from past wounding, but also from past unfulfilled emotional expectations. Yet this still is not enough. There is a third source of emotional pain: *habits*. Dealing with the negative habits spawned by emotional pain and wounding is the most crucial factor in conquering the *persisted* pain that plagues the heart.

### Habits

All of us have habits in our lives. We perform tasks without even focusing on or realizing what we are doing because we do it subconsciously, out of habit. Many of us do not realize that habits weave themselves throughout all four realms of our lives: mental, physical, spiritual and *emotional*. In other words, we each have certain and particular *mental* habits, *physical* habits, *spiritual* habits and *emotional* habits.

Our Creator intended habits to be developed in our lives to produce peace, love and joy, among other things. If not for the emotional pain living within many of us, habits that produce feelings of love, peace, joy, etc. would exist within, and dominate, our lives. Yet the emotional pain, when left unchecked, swims freely within the heart and alters our behavior. Our behavior is altered by *our reactions to the pain*. These reactions, when *repeated* several times, inevitably become a *habit*: a *mental* habit, a *physical* habit, a *verbal* habit, or an *emotional* habit. These habits created within us (from reaction to emotional pain felt and experienced throughout our lives) cause us to *think*, *say*, *feel* and *do* things that...

 ⇨ are not a reflection of our real personality,
 ⇨ actually set us up for more pain, and
 ⇨ make us feel that we are bad, weak, wicked, inferior or worthy of rejection by those around us.

Consequently, we fear that these feelings are a reflection of a dark, bad or inferior side of our heart (the monster we spoke of in Chapter One). This then leads us into feelings of confusion (Chapter Two). So, in order to experience genuine and permanent healing, freedom and release from fear, wounding and emotional pain, we have to deal with all three sources of our emotional pain.

In addition to this, we also must make sure we are using the right tools for the job. What do I mean by this? You will see as you read the next chapter.

*Remember & Reflect*   *In order to understand ourselves emotionally (and not react to confused feelings), it is important to remember that our emotional pain comes from three sources:*

> **wounding**,
> **unfulfilled emotional expectations**, *and*
> **habits**, *spawned by wounding and unfulfilled expectations.*

# CHAPTER 5

## *Emotional Healing & Change: Like Playing the Lottery?*
### *Why Our Attempts at Healing and Change Often Fail*

*W*hy is it that many of our attempts at emotional healing and change often come up short? Why can't there be permanent and genuine change with the negative, painful and life altering feelings we sometimes feel? When it comes to emotional healing and change, you can easily get the impression that it is like playing a game of chance: sometimes you win, sometimes you lose. At times, our attempts to experience emotional love, healing, freedom and peace cause us to feel as if we are playing a lottery—an emotional lottery!

### Using the Wrong Tools

Changes *can* be genuine and permanent if we use the appropriate tools for our emotional healing and change.

Most of our clients come to us having faced this frustrating dilemma. Before coming to The Life Institute, many have already tried many different tools and approaches in their quest for emotional love, healing, freedom and peace.

One such client, whom we will call Barbara, was an example of this. Barbara came to us with uncontrollable fear, anger and rage. These negative emotions were destroying every good relationship and job opportunity that entered her life.

For years, Barbara had tried to conquer these emotions. She had exhausted every tool known to man. She had been in and out of psychological therapy several times. She received treatment in a mental hospital on one occasion. She was on prescription medication for depression when we met her.

Barbara went through several spiritual processes as well. She tried a form of spiritual counseling referred to as "deliverance." She had also received extensive counseling from several ministers and spiritual counselors. Over the years, Barbara tried everything she knew to try.

At times, some of these tools and methods brought a measure of relief for Barbara. However, Barbara found that she was becoming dependent on her therapy sessions. She began feeling that she could not live without them. As soon as she stopped her sessions, the relief she had experienced left her.

Her experience with the psychiatric hospital did not help her at all. She said it only seemed to further her fears. Because of previous diagnoses from several "authorities" this experience left Barbara with even greater feelings of hopelessness. Others' diagnoses of her mental state made Barbara feel boxed in and confined. She said the diagnoses felt like labels she was destined to wear for life.

Drug medication did not deliver the changes Barbara was seeking, either. The drugs only seemed to numb Barbara's senses. As soon as the drugs wore off, the negative emotions flooded back, full throttle. To make matters even worse, by the time we met Barbara, she was dependent on her medication. Barbara had been taking the prescription for several years by the time she crossed our path.

Barbara's spiritual "deliverance" experience provided her with the greatest measure of relief she had ever experienced prior to coming to us. She even thought permanent changes had occurred.

Yet, several months later, the old feelings and fears resurfaced. Before long, Barbara's old emotional habit patterns were again in full swing.

Why hadn't any of these methods, approaches or tools for emotional healing and change worked for Barbara? Yes, they brought some measure of relief. A couple of the methods even gave her a temporary measure of felt change. However, none had brought *permanent* love, healing, freedom or peace. Why?

It was because the wrong tools were being used. Barbara's problems were *emotional* problems. They were not physical, mental or spiritual in nature (though these three areas were definitely affected by the *emotionally*-based problems). Consequently, what was needed was the use of *emotionally*-based tools and principles.

With this truth in mind, we began walking Barbara through a series of assignments that caused her to *feel* love. The love, in turn, heightened Barbara's sense of self-value, worth, and confidence. As these healthy emotions increased, Barbara's battles with fear, anger and rage subsided. Within a few months, Barbara improved to the point of being able to discontinue her medication as well.

### A House with Four Parts

Many of us often feel so hopeless over our emotional situation because we, and those aiding us, have been trying to bring about change with the wrong tools. From Chapter Two we learned that all of us have four distinct parts, or realms, to our human existence. We rarely take one of those realms, the *emotional-self*, into account. For ages, we have tried to work on the *emotional-self* with tools that were meant for the mind, body or spirit within us. Is this not correct? Think about it.

We usually try to accomplish genuine and permanent love, healing, freedom, peace and behavioral change within our lives by using physical, psychological or spiritual tools and principles. However, how many of us have used *emotionally*-based tools to remedy our emotional problems? Probably not too many. If we had used *emotionally*-based tools and principles, many more of us would be emotionally happy, whole, healed, free and at peace. We are not. Our families reflect this, our churches and synagogues reflect this, our cities and towns reflect this, and our society as a whole reflects this. All of human life reflects the fact that we are not happy, whole, healed, free or at peace.

To better understand this dilemma, picture your human entity (your body, spirit, mind and emotions) as a house (see Illus. 5–1).

Illus. 5-1: **A House With Four Parts.**

A house has *four* distinctively different, yet interrelated, parts or realms:

1. *The outside shell or structure.*
   This  protects and houses the other three realms or parts of the house.
2. *The plumbing.*
   This supplies the needed water system to the house. The plumbing serves as a *channel* to deliver and to extract water and water-based needs.
3. *The electrical system.*
   This supplies the *energy* and *power* to the house. Without the power, there would be no lights or functioning appliances.
4. *The climate comforts, or climate control.*  This controls the heating and air-conditioning.

In this day and age, most of us take the climate comfort for granted.  In doing so, we squabble, focus on and argue about which of the other three parts of the house is  the most important. Some will say the shell is the most important part of the house. Without it there would be no physical house.  Others convince themselves that the plumbing is the most important part of the house. Without it, there would be no water, plumbing, drainage or sewage system.  Still others would argue that the electrical system is by far the most important part of the house. Without it, there would be no energy,  power or light in times of darkness.

The fact is that all of these parts are vitally important.  However, when it comes to our own *felt* creature comfort and happiness, none is as important as the "climate control" of the house. Think about this for a moment.  How happy and comfortable would you *feel* if, in the dead of winter, you had no heat?  The temperature outside would be 15 degrees below zero, and you would  have no heat in your house.  How comfortable would you be?  How happy would you *feel*?

How comfortable would you feel if you were in the middle of summer with no air conditioning and the outdoor temperature was 100 degrees? Having no air-conditioning in your house, how well would you be able to sleep or rest at night? Not very well, right? So, whether we realize it or not, for most of us, climate control is far more important than the shell, the plumbing, or even the electrical portions of our house. When our climate control is broken or nonexistent, we subsequently do, say, think and feel some very irrational things, don't we?

### The Human "House"

Compare your human entity with a house: your body would be the shell of the house; your mind would be the plumbing; your spirit would be the electrical system; and your *emotional-*self would be the climate control (the heating and air conditioning).

| **House** | | **Human** |
|---|---|---|
| shell | ➤ | body |
| plumbing | ➤ | mind/will |
| electrical | ➤ | spirit |
| climate control | ➤ | *emotional*-self |

Now, with this idea in mind, how effective is it for you and me to accomplish a positive, genuine and permanent effect on the climate control of our "emotional" house if we are using tools and methods that are designed for the shell (our bodies) of the house alone—i.e., medicine or physical exercise?

How effective is it for you and me to accomplish a positive, genuine and permanent effect on the climate control of our "emotional" house if we are using tools and methods that are designed for the plumbing (our minds or intellects) alone—i.e., psychological tools?

How effective is it for you and me to accomplish a positive, genuine and permanent effect on the climate control of our "emotional" house if we are using tools and methods that are designed for the electrical system (our spirits) alone—i.e., spiritual tools?

Surely, using tools and methods designed for these three parts of our "emotional" house will help us at times. However, as you can see, it can be like playing a game of chance: sometimes you win, sometimes you lose. How is this so? Well, think about it for a moment. If I am attempting to experience genuine relief, change or repair of my emotional "climate control" system by working with tools for the trade of plumbing, I may, at times, fix the problem, or part of the problem. However, the repair will not be permanent. Such a repair will take place simply because there are times when my "climate control" problem may be related to or connected with a plumbing problem.

However, what happens when my climate control problem is not a plumbing problem in nature? What if the problem is electrical in nature? Or what if the climate control problem is a result of some defect with the physical structure or shell? If I continue to work with and repair my "climate control" with plumbing tools, I will, by chance, fix the problem, from time to time. Sometimes I will win with this approach. Sometimes I will lose.

### Using the Right Tools

When we attempt to fix, repair or change something, we should use the right tools for the job.

Yet, when it comes to our *emotional*-self, we often do not use the right tools. Most of the time, we will work with physical, mental, or spiritual tools and methods in an attempt to fix, repair, or change an *emotional* problem. Does this make sense? Can you see how we err? Can you see why so many of our past attempts fall short? It is because we often have been using the wrong tools.

This is also why our past attempts may have brought some measure of relief, but not genuine, permanent relief. We have been trying to repair or change our *emotional*-self (climate control) with tools and methods designed to work with the other three realms of our lives: the body (shell), the mind (plumbing), and the spirit (electrical). Since, by nature, all of these three involve and interrelate with the *emotional*-self (just as the shell, plumbing, and electrical system interrelate with the climate-control of a house), using the tools of the other three realms will sometimes help. However, the help or relief is usually only temporary at best. It definitely is a gamble, a game of chance. It will remain a gamble, too, until we know exactly what the problem is, *emotionally*, and which of the other three realms is involved. Only then will we know which tools will remedy the problem.

So why have so many of our past attempts at permanent and genuine love, healing, freedom, peace, relief or behavioral change failed? Often it is because we have attempted to do our repairs with the wrong tools for the job. Just as a house has four distinct, yet different parts, we too consist of different, yet interrelated parts. Consequently, when one part malfunctions, we will best be served if we will work with the tools and methods that are designed for the specific problem and part. If the problem is emotional, then emotional tools are best suited for the job.

At this point, we can clearly see how our past attempts at healing and change have missed their marks. We can also now see that maybe it *is* possible to change the way we feel, *if* we know *which* tools to work with—*emotionally*-based tools.

In the next chapter we will see the influence that external variables have on our *emotional*-self. We will also discuss our options in controlling our *emotional*-self as it reacts to those variables.

———————

*Remember & Reflect* **1.** *As our human entity consists of four parts, a house is also made up of four parts:*

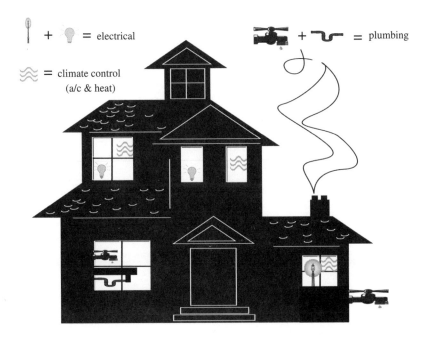

$\mathbf{|}$ + 💡 = electrical          + ⌐ = plumbing

≈ = climate control
(a/c & heat)

*Each part is uniquely different and distinct, yet interrelated.*

| <u>**House**</u> | | <u>**Human**</u> |
|---|---|---|
| *shell* | ➤ | *body* |
| *plumbing* | ➤ | *mind/will* |
| *electrical* | ➤ | *spirit* |
| *climate control* | ➤ | emotional-*self* |

2. *All too often, we try to fix, repair or change our **emotional**-self with tools and methods designed for one of the other three realms of our lives (physical, mental or spiritual).*

3. *When we approach our **emotional**-self in this way, it is like trying to repair the climate-control part of a house with tools designed only or specifically for the other three parts of a house: sometimes it works and sometimes it doesn't. Sometimes it works because the emotional problem is rooted in a plumbing (psychological), electrical (spiritual), or structural (physical/medical) factor, but sometimes it isn't. So, the wrong tools may, at times, work. But, not permanently.*

4. *When we attempt to fix, repair or change something, we should use the right tools for the job.*

# CHAPTER 6

## *Harnessing Your Greatest Power*
### *Learning to Control and Direct Your Emotions*

*W*ater is an incredible resource. Without it, there would be no life on earth. We are totally dependent on water for our survival. Yet, water also has the power to alter and even destroy. The power and force behind a river current can physically change the path of the river. The great Mississippi river of the United States is an example of this phenomenon. The "Mighty Mississippi" has changed its course, at differing junctions, throughout recorded and non-recorded history. Nothing and no one can stand in the path of a river when it decides to change its course.

The enormity and power of water generated attention during the summer of 1993. That year the weather patterns over the continent of North America were altered. This difference set off constant rain storms that deluged the U.S. Midwest for several weeks. This, coupled with the regular winter snow run-off from higher elevations into the "Mighty Mississippi," caused the Mississippi River to flood beyond its banks. Some called it the worst flood in 500 years!

In 1993 we learned that sometimes not even man's best engineering devices can dictate or direct the path and power of a channel of water. The Mississippi rose to a level far above flood stage. It engulfed man-made levies that had stood for decades. Whole towns were swallowed by its mighty power. No one could do anything except watch the river run its course. Everyone had to wait on the river. Finally, after several months, the river crested. Its waters receded. However, life never returned to normal for thousands of people. There was no more "normal." "Normal" was swept away by the power and might of the river.

Another dramatic example of water's force is seen with the Grand Canyon in the western region of the U.S. To view the Grand Canyon from the air is breathtaking. Within the Grand Canyon, the forces of water have left their footprints on the face of the Rocky Mountains. Those prints *are* the Grand Canyon. What other natural forces can manipulate and work rock into submission? Not many.

The floods that consumed the earth during the days of Noah are yet another example of water's power. Those floods are documented history. The wind and water that blasts shorelines and erodes top soil during a thunderstorm or hurricane are additional examples of water's strength.

Water has the power to destroy and produce change (sometimes unwanted change). Yet, when we learn the *mysteries* of the *power* behind water, when we learn how to harness, channel and direct this power, the results can produce good benefits for all.

One of the best examples of this is with the dam. Some of the biggest and greatest dams in the U.S. were built during the 1930's, the time of the Great Depression. These dams were built through government works programs. Dams, built properly, can harness and direct water's forces so as to provide better life styles for those fortunate enough to enjoy its benefit. Dams are used to produce lakes. Lakes, in turn, create opportunities for family and personal fun and recreation: swimming, boating, camping and fishing. Dams are used to create and provide electricity for the homes of millions of people. Lakes created by dams are used as municipal reservoirs for the water needs of a city or municipality.

Once we learn the secrets of water's power, we can learn to harness, channel and direct its energy for our desired good.

## The Greatest Power Within You

Emotions work in a very similar way to water. By far, they contain the greatest power within you. The power unleashed by your *emotional*-self *exceeds* the power of your body and your mind. You know this is true when you stop to think about it. Your body can not consistently dictate or control the rest of your being (your mind, emotions or spirit). Your mind can not consistently dictate or control your entire being, either. However, your emotions *regularly* do control, dictate and influence the other areas of your being. Your *emotional*-self is powerful enough to make you do (through your body), say (through your mouth), and think (through your mind) things that sometimes are not what you want. The emotions can make you produce behavior that you disdain, yet feel powerless to change. On the other hand, emotions can control and influence the other three realms of your life in a way that produces love, healing, freedom, peace and happiness. It is actually up to you and me as to which way the forces of emotions flow within our lives. I know this statement may sound unfathomable, but it is true. *You can control, influence and direct the course that your feelings and emotions take.* The key is to learn the *mysteries* behind the forces and powers that make up your emotions and your *emotional*-self.

The reason so many of us are so afraid of our emotions is because we do not *understand* them (as discussed in both Chapters One and Two). We know of and are fully aware of their power, usually from destructive displays in our pasts. So we try to dismiss the *emotional*-self altogether. Consequently, we deny ourselves the benefits and fruits of what our Creator intended for us through good, fulfilling emotions in our lives.

It is time to move away from a perspective of fear, confusion and apprehension. It is time to gain an understanding of our emotions. We do not have to be held prisoner by this incredible power for the rest of our lives.

### Four Principles That Govern Your *Emotional*-Self

How do your emotions work? What are the mysteries behind their power? We will discover the answers to these questions in Parts II and III of this book. First, however, it is important that you and I understand four truths, or principles, that govern our *emotional*-self:

   **1**. You *can not* conquer emotions, but you *can* control and
        direct them.
   **2**. Emotions are *reactive*, not proactive.
   **3**. You must have an attitude of being *responsible* and in
        control of your *emotional*-self .
   **4**. You *can* acquire *understanding* as to how your emotions
        work.

### You Can Learn to Control Your Emotions

*You can not conquer emotions, but you can control them.*

As with water, the forces and powers that make up the *emotional*-self are far too great to conquer. But also like water, emotions can be harnessed, channeled, directed and therefore, controlled. You *can* learn to control your emotions in order to gain your desired outcome or benefit. *The more you learn, know and understand about your emotions and your **emotional**-self, the easier it will be to harness, control and direct this powerful aspect of your life.*

In order to gain a healthy control of your *emotional*-self three hurdles must be conquered:

*healing,*

*habits,*

*habitat*—the people, places and events around you.

### *Healing.*

There can be no control over raging, powerful emotions if there is no healing. Your heart, or *emotional*-self, must experience genuine love, healing, freedom, peace and release from the negative *effects* of all past wounding in your life (remember Chapters Three and Four). This sounds like a tall order. It is not. It is possible to be free from the powerful effects that your past wounding has had on your heart, mind and life.

### *Habits.*

In order to acquire a healthy control of your emotions, you must also be willing to conquer and replace many old, negative and destructive habits that have developed over the years. These habits usually have developed as a result of *repeated reactions* to your personal wounding and pain. The habits are usually in all four areas of your life: mental, emotional, physical and verbal. Such habits include:

*How you regularly react to those around you (physically, mentally and verbally);*

*The thoughts you regularly think about others or yourself;*

*The words that regularly come out of your mouth;* and

*The feelings you regularly feel when in certain environments.*

### Conquering Bad Habits

Habits are hard to break. We can not break or change habits by focusing on them. As a matter of fact, the more you focus on a habit, the more entrenched it becomes within your life style. The only way to genuinely and permanently conquer a habit is by *replacing* it. You replace an old habit with a new one. So, you must focus on a new habit being formulated within your being. As you do this, the new habit replaces the old one, permanently.

How do we create new habits? By repetition. That is how the old habit was established and created in the first place.

The more times you think a thought, do a deed, speak a word, or feel a feeling, the greater the likelihood that it will become a habit. So, choose what you wish to become a habit, and begin repeating it often; whether mentally, verbally, physically or emotionally.

Years ago, I came across a catchy phrase that seems to make habit formation a fun and positive exercise:

> *Sow a thought, reap a deed,*
> *Sow a deed, reap a habit,*
> *Sow a habit, reap a destiny.*

Many of us are familiar with the negative consequences of this process. So let's turn it around and apply it as a force and influence for positive and healthy healing and change for our lives. Try it. It works. Replace a habit this week!

### *Habitat.*

Do you ever feel a heaviness after spending time with certain friends or relatives? Do you find yourself feeling that you should be more of something than you are when you are around them? Do you find yourself feeling that you don't or can't measure up to their expectations?

If you answer yes to any of these questions, it may be that you are trying to fit in and please the external environment you are in—your friendships and relationships.

In order for you to acquire a good, positive, and healthy control of your *emotional*-self, you may have to change your external environment as well. If, after having accomplished the first two hurdles mentioned above (healing and habits), you still find yourself being pulled or influenced in a negative, destructive or defeating way by the externals around you, then your only alternative may be to change where you live, or where you work, or with whom you keep company. The external influences *will* affect your internal being. The old adages, "You are known for the company you keep," and "You become what you are around," are Biblical principles. They are also very true. So, it is to your advantage to place yourself around externals that will *affirm* and *strengthen* your *emotional*-self and who you are as a person. Sometimes this means making some very hard and difficult decisions, especially with the company you keep. However, sometime in your life you may have to choose: "Which is more important to me, my hopes (hope in a given relationship, job, activity or environment), or my peace?" It is your choice.

It is important to remember, though, that *this hurdle can not be crossed before the first two are crossed.* This step can not be taken to simply *flee* a situation. It must be done solely because you are *first* already a happy, healed and emotionally free person, but you realize that your current environment is a serious threat to the continuation of your emotional love, healing, freedom and peace.

Once you have experienced genuine love, healing, freedom and peace, take control of your external environment as well. Choose the friends, neighborhood, activities and vocation that best *fits you* and your heart nature. Don't spin your wheels trying to *fit in*. Let things *fit you*. There are hundreds of thousands of friends, neighborhoods, activities and vocations in this world. There are over *six billion* people on this earth. So surely, there are some places, vocations and people out there that will *fit you* and your particular heart-nature—as long as your heart is whole, healed, free and healthy.

How can you be in control of your *emotional*-self? By orchestrating three factors in your life to best work *for* you, not against you. Those three factors are *healing*, *habits* and *habitat*.

### Your Emotions React to External Variables
*Emotions are reactive.*

Your *emotional*-self was created as a *reactive* unit. It is not *proactive*. What does this mean? It means that your *emotional*-self is *not* an "advanced action unit." It doesn't lead or initiate. Your *emotional*-self *follows*. It *reacts* or *responds* to the lead of some other internal or external stimulus. That stimulus may be an action, a word, or even a thought. The stimulus may have originated *from* you, or from some other person or event *outside* of you. However, your emotions and your *emotional*-self are reactive, not proactive.

Our mind and body can be either reactive or proactive. All too often, though, we allow the mind and body to be reactive. We allow them to be controlled and influenced by the fears, feelings and emotions produced by our wounded-self.

Your *emotional*-self is always in a constant flux of reacting to the things, people and events around you. *Your* emotional-*self reacts to spoken words perceived and received.* Think about this for a moment. It is true, isn't it? Your *emotional*-self is always reacting to what your eyes and ears are taking in. Good or bad, positive or negative, your *emotional*-self reacts to what is perceived and received. It is that simple. Your *emotional*-self is a follower, not a leader. However, when left unbridled, because it has so much power, it can cause you to do, say, think and feel things that are sometimes not a reflection of the real you, but reflect the wounded you. Consequently, through *reactions*, your *emotional*-self can and often does stimulate, direct and control subsequent mental, emotional, verbal and physical reactions within you.

This then gives you the feeling and impression that your *emotional*-self is, indeed, leading. It is not. It may be *directing* (as a consequence of reacting to some other stimulus), and it may be *controlling*. But your *emotional*-self is *not leading*. It is following, but because of its tremendous power, it causes the rest of your being to follow its whim.

The point is, if emotions are reactive, then it is possible to influence, direct, channel, control and even harness the external variables that your emotions *react* to. This can be accomplished in such a way as to direct and predict your emotions' future reactions. In order to do this, you must first have a balanced life style: you must first bring your emotions into balance. As previously mentioned, emotions are balanced as you reckon with three factors in your emotional life: *healing*, *habits* and *habitat*.

### Have An Attitude of Responsibility

*You must be in control and responsible for your feelings.*

As we learned from Chapter Three, emotions (especially wounded emotions) are something that come upon you, from within you. They are not necessarily a part of you. Nor are they necessarily a reflection of you. This sounds very irresponsible, doesn't it? On the contrary. You must be willing to accept this fact and take responsibility for, and control of, your emotions and *emotional*-self in order to have a chance to harness and channel this enormous power within you.

It is impossible to control and harness your *emotional*-self if you have a mindset of blaming others, or holding others responsible for who you are, how you feel, or for the circumstances surrounding your life. If you are living your life blaming or holding others responsible for your feelings and life, you have given those people control of your *emotional*-self. Consequently, you are bombarded with thoughts and feelings of "no control," or having "no say-so" in who you are or how you feel. You are swept away by feelings that "others have more of a control over my feelings than I do."

The fact is, you gave others that control when you chose not to take responsibility and control for who you were or how you felt. *You gave up control when you chose to blame, look to, hope in, or hold others responsible for your life and feelings.* When this happens, it places you at the threshold of fear, hopelessness and depression. Can you see this? This is why it is vitally important for you:

⇨ to be in charge;

⇨ to take control of your *emotional*-self;

⇨ to take control of your external environment (relationships, jobs, activities, etc.); and

⇨ to take responsibility for who you are and how you feel.

### Don't Look For an Emotional Savior

Most of us would rather blame others than take control and responsibility for our thoughts and feelings. Why? Because we want a savior.  We are all looking for a savior.  We are not necessarily looking for a spiritual savior, but an *emotional* savior:

Someone who will *rescue* us.  Someone who will *nurture* us.
Someone who will *affirm* us.  Someone who will *accept* us.
Someone who will *validate* us.  Someone who will *love* us.
Someone who will *help* us to feel good about ourselves.

In essence, we want to return to the safety and warmth of the womb—no responsibility, no cares, no hassles, someone else always covering for us.  Sounds great, doesn't it?  No, it does not!  Many of us do not realize that when we are in this state of existence, our heart has no way of verifying or affirming its strengths, gifting or abilities.  Consequently, it is unable to produce self-confidence, value or worth.

At this point, we begin to look to others to give us a sense of confidence, value or worth in ourselves.  When we try this approach (of looking to others for our sense of confidence, value or worth), we always lose.  This approach always comes up short.  Why?  Often the people whom we are looking to for validation have wounded hearts themselves.  Consequently, they too are more focused on getting and receiving, not on giving and validating.  When you seek an emotional savior outside of yourself, chances are that your self-confidence, value and worth will remain extremely low, and almost always it will even diminish.

An increased self-confidence, value or worth only comes when your heart, nature and character are forced to plow through the challenges and fears you face in life.  When you victoriously walk through these challenges and fears, your self-esteem increases.

You might say,

*"But what if I fail?"*

It is this very attitude and approach that insures your failure!  How?  Because the thought of failure rivets your focus *on* failure.  Another Biblical principle states:

**"What I always feared has happened to me."**
**The Bible**

This can mean that when we focus on a fear, we become pre-occupied with that fear. When we are preoccupied with a fear we end up doing, saying, and thinking things that are more influenced by the fear, rather than by our own heart-nature. Once our behavior is being controlled by the thought of the fear, dynamics start working within our lives that allow the fear to "come to pass," to happen or occur. Do you see how this happens? It works on all of us. This dynamic is universal.

A good example of this principle being played out is with the fear of rejection:

⇨ *I fear that I will be rejected as I enter a room and interact with a group of people.*

➠ *I then become preoccupied with the fear of being rejected.*

➠ *Before I know it, I am convinced that I will be rejected (though I still haven't been rejected).*

➠ *At this point, being so preoccupied (mentally and emotionally) with the fear of being rejected, I take on a peculiar behavior while around those in the group.*

➠ *My odd behavior becomes obvious to all.*

➠ *They respond with skeptical caution.*

➠ *As I sense their caution, I feel their apprehension.*

➠ *I conclude that they are, in fact, rejecting me, just as I had suspected they would.*

➠ *Then, I react with another, deliberate, negative, more rejecting behavior, while I conclude within myself that they did as I suspected. They rejected me.*

*Before I know it, without realizing it, I have sealed my own fate. My preoccupation with my own fear brought the fear upon me.*

Do you see how that happens? It happens to all of us in every area of our lives—relationally, vocationally, financially, spiritually—every area!

Frankly, there is no way you can fail to gain emotional healing and change as long as you don't give up, quit or look to someone else to be your emotional savior. It just doesn't happen. In other words, *failure does not occur when you are taking on an attitude of control and responsibility for your life and feelings.*

### See Your Mistakes As Stepping Stones, Not Failures

This is not to say that you will not make mistakes. You probably will. But mistakes are not necessarily failures. Quitting or giving up—that is a failure. A wrong decision or a mistaken action is not necessarily a failure. Society may label it a failure. It is not. If you can and do learn from the mistake, it is not a failure. *It is a stepping stone toward eventual success.*

This was the attitude that brought Abraham Lincoln to the presidency. Prior to his presidential victory, Mr. Lincoln ran in and lost two elections for Congressional seats. Not only that, but the man who ran against him for the presidency, Stephen Douglas, was the very same person who defeated him in his two previous defeats for Congress. Think about this for a moment. Put yourself in President Lincoln's shoes. He had every right to feel like a failure, to feel as though he had made a mistake by running for public office, not once, but twice. *And with feelings of failure comes quitting, giving up.* So by today's standards, he should have given up long before he ran for president.

Think of where our country would be today if he had not run for president. He held this country together when it was at the brink of destruction. You and I have multiple blessings and opportunities today because one man chose not to see his defeats as failures or mistakes, but as stepping stones toward eventual success.

Any meaningful success in life is almost always accompanied by many previous wrong turns or mistakes. Through our mistakes, we learn how to do it correctly *the next time*. Success is inevitable when we use this approach with emotions and relationships. If you don't believe this, challenge it. Put it to the test. Try it for thirty days. Determine not to quit or give up for thirty days. The results will surprise you. I see it verified constantly and consistently with those going through our counseling/life-improvement process.

### You *Can* Understand Your Emotions

*You can gain understanding behind the mystery of how your emotions work.*

You *can* understand how you feel the things you feel. First, though, you must be willing to accept and abide by the first three truths discussed in this chapter:

*1. You* can not *conquer emotions, but you* **can** *control them.*

*2. Emotions are* reactive, ***not*** *proactive.*

*3. You must be willing to take personal* **responsibility** *for your* **emotional**-*self.*

Are you willing to work within the perimeters of these truths? If so, continue on. The remainder of this book gives you an understanding into the mysteries behind your emotions and how they work.

In Part II, we will look at our emotions from the viewpoint of wounding. You will learn how wounding affects and even alters your behavior (mentally, emotionally, physically and spiritually). You will learn how emotional wounding often creates the destructive habits that seem to place a dark cloud over certain areas of your life (feelings, thoughts, relationships, jobs, finances, etc.).

In Part III we will explore the whole and healed *emotional*-self. It is a reflection of what your Creator intended for you, from the womb, before wounding set in and altered your thoughts, feelings and behavior.

———— ▯ ————

*Remember*
*& Reflect*

1. Your **emotional**-self is a great and mighty **power** within your being.

2. You can not conquer that power, but you can learn to **control** it, once you properly factor in these three variables in your life:
   **healing**,
   **habits** and
   **habitat**.

3. Emotions are **reactive**, not proactive.

4. You must have an approach and attitude of **taking responsibility** for, and being in control of, your **emotional**-self; otherwise, you will fail.

5. You **can** gain understanding behind the mystery of how your emotions work.

# Review

# Part I

Before moving on to "Part II: The Wounded-Self," let's review what we have already discussed.

### Chapter One:

## *Your Wounded-Self vs. Your Real-Self*

### *Living A Masked Life*

1. Because of wounding and the fear that our *real*-self may be bad, evil, defective, inferior or wicked, many of us adopt a masked life approach to living.
2. When unaffected by wounding and unaffected by the negative influences of others around us, most of us are loving, kind and warmhearted. We are good people, with tender, caring hearts.
3. In order to experience emotional healing and change, you first must get to know and understand your *emotional*-self.

### Chapter Two:

## *Who Are You?*

### *An Entity Consisting of Four Parts*

1. A lack of understanding with regard to our emotions and our *emotional*-self, produces confusion.
2. By nature, we focus our attention on the feelings and thoughts of confusion (the fruit) and thereby react to them, rather than trying to understand where they come from (the root).
3. By design, your human entity consists of four distinct parts, or realms: a body, a spirit, a mind/will and an *emotional*-self.
4. It is important that we learn to perceive life from an *emotional* perspective rather than a physical, mental (intellectual) or spiritual perspective. We will approach the remainder of our discussions in this book from the *emotional* perspective.

### Chapter Three:

## *How wounding Works*

### *The Anatomy of a Wart*

1. As with the plantar wart, *external* feelings, fears and emotions are *triggered* by deeply rooted internal *emotional* wounding.

2.  External invaders (wounding) can and do *alter* your mental, emotional, physical and verbal behavior.

3.  How you *react* to the externals in your life (the relationships, jobs and events around you), determines your level of emotional love, freedom, peace and happiness.

4.  Emotional wounding triggers *pain*;
    >you *react* to the pain;
    >>when repeated often enough,
    >>>your reactions become *habit*.

5.  These habits are directly determined by how you *react* to the wounding, inwardly within yourself, and outwardly toward those around you.

6.  All of the negative thoughts, feelings, words and actions that come out of you are *not* a reflection of the *real* you. They are a reflection of the *wounded* you.

## Chapter Four:

# *Three Sources of Emotional Pain*
### *Where Wounding Comes From*

In order to *understand* ourselves emotionally (and not *react* to confused feelings), it is important to remember that our emotional pain comes from three sources:

>*wounding*,

>*unfulfilled emotional expectations*, and

>*habits*, spawned by wounding and unfulfilled expectations.

## Chapter Five:

# *Emotional healing & Change:*
# *Like Playing the Lottery?*
### *Why Our Attempts at Healing & Change Often Fail*

1. As our human entity consists of four parts, a house is also made up of four parts:

*Each part is uniquely different and distinct, yet interrelated.*

| House | | Human |
|---|---|---|
| shell | ➤ | body |
| plumbing | ➤ | mind/will |
| electrical | ➤ | spirit |
| climate control | ➤ | *emotional*-self |

2. All too often, we try to fix, repair or change our *emotional*-self with tools and methods designed for one of the other three realms of our lives (physical, mental or spiritual).

3. When we approach our *emotional*-self in this way, it is like trying to repair the climate-control part of a house with tools designed only or specifically for the other three parts of a house: sometimes it works and sometimes it does not. Sometimes it works because the emotional problem is rooted in a plumbing (psychological), electrical (spiritual), or structural (physical/medical) factor, but sometimes it is not. So, the wrong tools may, at times, work. But, not permanently.

4. When we attempt to fix, repair or change something, we should use the right tools for the right job.

**Chapter Six:**

## *Harnessing Your Greatest Power*
### *Learning to Control and Direct Your Emotions*

1. Your *emotional*-self is a great and mighty *power* within your being.

2. You can not conquer that power, but you can learn to *control* it, once you properly factor in these three variables in your life:
   *healing*,
   *habits*, and
   *habitat*.

3. Emotions are *reactive*, not proactive.

4. You must have an approach and attitude of *taking responsibility* for, and being in control of, your *emotional*-self; otherwise, you will fail.

5. You *can* gain understanding behind the mystery of how your emotions work.

# Part II

## The Wounded-Self

*"Above all else, guard your heart,*
*for it influences everything else in your life."*

\* \* \* \* \*

*"A tree is identified by its fruit.*
*A tree from a select variety produces good fruit;*
*poor varieties don't."*

**The Bible**

# CHAPTER 7

# *An Invasion of the Heart*
## *The Emotional-Self is Like a Tree*

$\mathcal{I}$f there is a hell on earth, this is it. Most of us have tasted this hell. It may have been thrust upon you as a one-time, devastating occurrence. Usually though, it creeps in over the years—slowly—eating away at your heart and altering every fiber of your being.

It may start out as a feeling of being abandoned or rejected, or a fear of being inferior or inadequate. Or it may begin as the result of some major, traumatic event (such as a death, divorce or abuse).

Regardless of how it begins, it inevitably alters and changes what you do, say, think and feel. It robs you of your pleasure for life. It causes you to fear, question or doubt your own instincts and insights. It produces an emotional hell.

## My Own Masked Life

By my seventeenth year, I was well acquainted with the wounded-self. I had developed an elaborate masked life.

During my adolescent years, I had created many habits that eventually shut down my *emotional*-self. These mechanisms were an attempt to numb the hurt, wounding and pain that were my constant, internal, emotional companions.

At seventeen, I could look back on my life and see that plenty of signs had surfaced during my young life that were indications, or maybe warnings, that something was out of balance.

⇨ After keeping me with him each summer, my father would bring me back home to live with my mother. Upon my return, I would go immediately to my bedroom and cry, in heaves, for hours. The emotional pain of his lost presence in my life was devastating. The crying spells lasted for three to five hours. When they came, I could not physically stop them or shut them off. No matter how much I determined that the emotions would not surface, the pain and tears always overpowered me and my willed determination. Totally against my personal strength and resolve, the emotions and tears that were triggered by my father's departure at the end of each summer became a routine in my life. These uncontrollable outbursts caused me to question and doubt myself, my strength, my stability, and even my manhood.

⇨ When I was in elementary school, the teachers, the principal and my mother seemed to constantly have conferences. I knew something was going on, but I didn't know what they were discussing. My mother said that I had an attention deficit problem. She said my grades were not reflective of my IQ. She expressed to me what was apparently everyone's bewilderment about the problem.

All I knew was that life was difficult, empty, lonely and painful. I just wanted to run away. I wanted to be somewhere else; I didn't know where. Just some place where the hurt, pain and loneliness would not be with me.

⇨ When I was nine, my mother frequently took me to the doctor. It turned out that I had an ulcer. I remember thinking, "What's an ulcer?" I was told it was like a cut or wound on the inner wall of my stomach. I learned that it was the result of emotional anxiety and tension. I knew only two things:

1. Wow! I wasn't hiding the emotional pain and grief very well, and
2. No more fried chicken or hamburgers for a while (for two years, which was an eternity at the age of nine)!

### The Beginning of My Emotional Transformation

By my seventeenth year, my emotional turmoil seemed to climax. I had developed an internal life style that denied and suppressed anger, anxiety, fear, depression, rejection and performance-based living. Internally, I was blaming others for my predicament. I had a difficult time respecting authority, and my attitude toward my Creator was not the greatest.

By the end of my seventeenth year, these feelings began to change. In April of 1975 I experienced what many would consider a religious or spiritual experience. For me, it was much more than that. It was the beginning of an *emotional* transformation. For the first time since my preschool years, I felt someone loved me and accepted me *unconditionally* for who I was. That Someone was my Creator. His love swept through my entire being. It was like a new life. It was a new beginning to life, a fresh new start. It was great. My Creator's love for me was what the doctor should have ordered.

Questions and issues arose as a result of this new love and life:

➪ *How was it that I had not felt or received any unconditional love or acceptance all those years?*

➪ *Why, even with this new life, did I still have reoccurrences of the old, negative thoughts, feelings, fears and actions that had developed during my adolescent years?*

➪ *Why was it that those old thoughts, feelings, fears and actions seemed to regularly smother the new love I had encountered through my spiritual transformation?*

These and other questions led me on my own emotional Journey toward love, healing, freedom and peace. Through this Journey, I learned that the love probably had been there all along. Yet, because of my wounding and pain, I was blinded to that love. *My wounding short-circuited my ability to* **receive** *love,* **perceive** *love,* **feel** *love, or even* **give** *love.* For years I blamed this on those around me. But the problem was not in them. It was in me. The wounding and pain *blinded* me. This blinding subsequently hindered me from receiving what was mine: unconditional love and acceptance.

However, even with these newly felt emotions of unconditional love and acceptance, some pre-existing and harmful mental, emotional, verbal and physical habits lingered around and consistently resurfaced. The habits were mental *thoughts,* emotional *feelings,* verbal *phrases,* and physical *actions.* Why hadn't the new experiences of love changed these habits? Was God not big enough? Maybe my spiritual experience and transformation were not real. Maybe even God had rejected me. Maybe I was a lost cause.

Even though I had these thoughts, I was not willing to give up on myself—not yet, anyway. Even with the self-doubts and conflicting emotions (such as feeling love and anger simultaneously), I had a deep inner feeling that I was *worthy* to be happy and healed. I felt *qualified* to live a peaceful, fulfilling life. These feelings supplied me with the drive and motivation to pursue peace and not give up on myself.

I now realize that part of this inner drive and belief in myself came from my Creator. However, an equally great portion of it came from my mother. In my early childhood, she had always affirmed me. Her words validated a deep inner sense of her belief and confidence in me. This never left me, even during the painful years. This is one of the reasons why I believe mothers can be the greatest gift on earth. The mothering we receive can determine much of our emotional life style.

In my quest to understand the new conflicts within myself (the conflicts between the old and the new *emotional*-self), I realized and discovered many things about a person's *emotional*-self. Three of those discoveries are:

   *1. Emotional feelings are universal; they are common to all of us.*

2. *Most of our inner conflicts and problems stem from our* **emotional**-*self and, therefore, are* **emotional in nature**, *not physical, spiritual or psychological.*
3. *Like a tree, the* **emotional**-*self is a multi-level, multi-sectioned entity within each of us.*

### Emotions are Universal

The feelings, fears and emotions we experience are, for the most part, universal. That is, you and I do not feel and experience feelings, fears or emotions that are uniquely ours alone.

While your emotions are not unique, the things, people or events that *trigger* your feelings, fears and emotions may be unique to you.

How you *respond* to the things, people and events that trigger your fears, feelings and emotions may also be unique to you.

In addition, the *experiences* that ushered in your wounding and pain may be unique to you.

However, the actual feelings, fears and emotions that you consequently feel and experience are universal, or common and similar, to us all. We all experience the same fears, feelings and emotions, even though the wounding or circumstances that trigger them, and how we respond to the wounding, may be unique to each of us. This realization is important.

When most of us are in a wounded state of existence, we feel and think that we are alone. We become convinced that there is no one around who will or can understand us and how we feel. This simply is not true. Others may not be able to identify with the *experiences* that triggered our pain. Yet, often, many can identify with our feelings, fears and emotions that the emotional wounding triggers.

Most of the time, however, we do not identify (we can, but we don't) with the emotions of those around us. This is because our personal focus is riveted on our own problems and pain, our own fears, feelings and emotions. Our attention, consequently, is distracted by a preoccupation with our own wounding or fear.

This, in turn, renders us incapable of being able to love, understand, support and lend healing to those around us.

However, when we are not distracted by our own fear, wounding and pain, we have the ability to understand, know and feel what others are going through and experiencing emotionally. We can do this because emotional feelings are universal.

### Most Inner Problems are Emotional

Most of our inner conflicts and problems stem from our *emotional*-self and, therefore, are *emotional* in nature, not physical, spiritual or psychological.

Blindness to this truth has caused so much misunderstanding, hurt and disappointment for many of us in our quest for love, healing, freedom and peace. By habit, we attempt to understand or comprehend life through the physical, mental or spiritual realms. Consequently, most of us try to address and effect *emotional* change through one of these three aspects of life. This approach sometimes brings relief. However, as we learned in Chapter Five, for most people, the relief is only temporary. Usually, the emotional relief lasts only until some external event comes along that again triggers the old fears and feelings.

The process that led you and me into our wounded emotional state of existence was an *emotional* process. For most of us, the digression was not physical, mental or spiritual. Therefore, we must go through a reversal of sorts, *emotionally*, in order to produce permanent emotional healing, freedom, peace and change from within. We must backtrack to the point where our emotional life strayed off course—the place and time where the wounding began. This is the place where we first lost touch with our *real*-self and became preoccupied with our *wounded*-self. Starting at that point, we need to remove, replace or repair the emotional roadblocks and barriers (the wounding) that originally took us off course, emotionally.

This is not to say that we need to unearth old or painful memories or emotional baggage. We simply need to locate the point in which we were distracted by the wounding and pain, the point where we stumbled off of the intended road or path for our emotional life. This is the place where our mental, physical, verbal and emotional behavior began to change. It is the "root" or starting point of our altered, wounded emotional life style. It is at this point where we can "repair the breach" in our behavior. Anything other than this will always come short of genuine and permanent change, healing, freedom and peace.

### Our *Emotional*-Self is Like a Tree

Like a tree the *emotional*-self is a multi-level, multi-sectioned entity within each of us. Our *emotional*-self isn't just an entity filled with space, like a ball. It is more like a tree, consisting of specific, yet varied levels or sections (see Illus. 7–1).

Illus. 7–1: **Ball and Tree**

A tree has several levels or *sections*. Each section has a specific *function*. Each section, doing its part, produces the *next* section:

The root produces the trunk.
The trunk produces the branches.
The branches produce the fruit.

So, from seed, to sapling, to succulent fruit, the tree goes through a process of *constant change*, from one section to the next, before arriving at the fruit. The *emotional*-self is very similar to a tree.

From my own Journey out of wounding and into love, healing, freedom and peace, I learned that feelings of fear, anger, depression, rejection, anxiety, performance-oriented living and other negative emotions did not just appear out of empty space. A negative and destructive emotional metamorphosis, or transformation, influenced by wounding and pain, took place. This transforming change began at the point in time of my initial wounding, which became the "root" of my wounded-self.

In other words, the outward expressions or "fruit" may have been fear, anger or depression. However, these were only the outward "fruits." They *reflected* and were the *results of* a deeper, inner "root." The "root" then set off a cycled process, or chain reaction, of negative and destructive feelings and attitudes that were totally contrary to my heart-nature.

As the emotional metamorphosis or transformation progressed, my behavior changed, and not for the better. The metamorphosis changed much of my mental, emotional, verbal and physical behavior. These changes were repeated often, and soon became habits. Consequently, they became part of my behavioral life style.

But where did it all begin? How was I transformed from a happy, pleasant person into a person with a life style of fear, anger, depression, rejection and performance-oriented living? What was the "root" cause of all of this?

The answers came, oddly enough, from a Bible. It was a Bible called *The Living Bible*. As I mentioned earlier, my spiritual encounter was much more than just a spiritual experience. It was an *emotional* experience as well. I experienced a felt unconditional love and acceptance that I never had experienced up to that point in my life. This love changed my life. It set me on a Journey of emotional and habit transformation and change.

With this, I discovered that the Bible was much more than a religious book. I saw the Bible as an *emotional manual* for life and living. So much of what I read in the Bible seemed to speak of *emotions*. Good or bad, right or wrong, weak or strong, emotional expressions were mentioned often in the Bible. A part of the Bible titled Romans spoke of being able to experience *peace, love* and *joy*. Another section of the Bible, Galatians, spoke of nine emotional expressions as though they were attainable:

> **"But when the Holy Spirit controls our lives he will produce this kind of fruit: love, joy, peace, patience, kindness, goodness, faithfulness, gentleness, and self-control."**
>
> **The Bible**

As I read these, I could *feel* what it would be like:

to *feel* love;

to *feel* peace;

to *feel* gentleness;

to *feel* self-control; and more.

Could this be possible? Was this stuff really attainable? I wanted it!

I also discovered things in the Bible that helped me relate to the hurt and pain I had experienced:

> **"My eyes are red from weeping; my health is broken from sorrow. I am pining away with grief. My years are shortened, drained away because of sadness."**
>
> **"He heals the broken hearted, binding up their wounds."**
>
> **The Bible**

This emotional manual, the Bible, became the manual for my emotional change, healing, freedom and peace. With it, I learned that my *emotional*-self, in a way similar to a tree, was multi-sectioned, multi-leveled. My *emotional*-self, when broken down into parts, could be said to consist of a *root*, a *trunk*, *branches* and *fruit*. This helped me a lot. It brought instant understanding to much of what I had felt and experienced all of my life. I learned that my *emotional* "tree," from the womb, was created in a certain and particular way, for a certain and particular function. That original function and purpose was good, positive and healthy.

Before wounding has an opportunity to disrupt the created intentions, our emotional "tree," by design, produces emotional feelings and expressions of love, freedom, peace and joy. We discuss this in greater detail beginning in Chapter Fifteen.

However, for the next few chapters we will concentrate our attention on the negative change and transformation that occurs within our *emotional*-self when wounding "roots" in and takes control.

In Chapter Eight we will probe the root, or starting point of the wounding process. Chapter Nine will help us see how wounding transforms itself from hurt and pain into thoughts and feelings of bitterness, self-centeredness and rebellion—or self-denial & compliance. In Chapter Ten we will see how the wounding manifests itself through our outward behavior. Chapters Eleven through Thirteen will show us how wounding affects the three major "branches" or areas of relationships in our lives. Chapter Fourteen will conclude this section of *A Journey to The Other Side of Life* with three real-life examples of how this wounding process can affect the *emotional*-self.

---

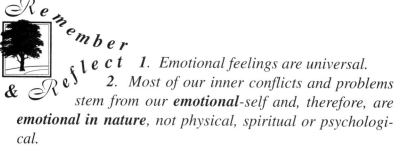

               *1. Emotional feelings are universal.*
               *2. Most of our inner conflicts and problems stem from our **emotional**-self and, therefore, are **emotional in nature**, not physical, spiritual or psychological.*

*3. Like a tree, the **emotional**-self is a multi-level, multi-sectioned entity within each of us.*

*4. An emotional metamorphosis begins within us when wounding enters our lives.*

# CHAPTER 8

# *Where It All Began: The Root*
## *The Wounded Spirit*

*W*ounding and fear usually enter most of us at an early age. At that point, they set off a metamorphic, life-altering, progressive change within the heart, or *emotional*-self. This change or process ultimately leads to some very negative and destructive emotional and behavioral changes. Most of us are well aware of many of these changes: anger, anxiety, fear, rejection, depression, performance-oriented living and abusiveness, to name a few.

When wounding enters our lives, through whatever circumstances, it "roots" into the core of our *emotional*-self, or heart. I refer to this "rooting" experience as a *wounded spirit*. The by-product of this experience is a wounded *emotional*-self. I refer to the wounded *emotional*-self as the *wounded*-self (see Illus. 8–1 on page 102).

A wounded spirit is what makes most of us join the ranks of the walking wounded. We do all that we can to dismiss it, deny

# The Wounded *Emotional*-Self

Illus. 8–1:  **The Wounded *Emotional*-Self**

it, cover it up or forget about it. However, for most of us, the emotional wound (and its life altering effect) is always there. The wound reveals its presence through our behavior: mentally, emotionally, verbally and physically.

### What Is A Wounded Spirit?

What is a "wounded spirit"? First, it is *not* a spiritual term. It is an *emotional* term. The word "spirit" in the term "wounded spirit" is not in reference to the God-given spirit that lies within you. In this instance, the term "spirit" refers to that *emotional* part of you that gives you your zest and zeal for life and living. It is the *emotional* part of you that produces your liveliness and vitality. It is the core of your *emotional*-self. It is your *heart*.

When wounding comes in, it crushes your heart. The spirit, or liveliness within you, dies. It drains you of your life and vitality. It can even rob you of your will to live. A place in the Bible called Proverbs speaks of this:

> **"Gentle words are a *tree of life,*
> but harsh words *crush the spirit.*"**
> **The Bible**

How does this happen? It happens when the wounding enters your life. It feels like an *invasion* or *violation* of your personhood. You did not ask for it. You did not invite it in. It was thrust upon you, sometimes violently, always painfully. When the wounding occurs, it feels as if your freedom is being stolen, or at the very least, threatened.

Before the wounding invades your life, your desire is simply to live, love, enjoy, be yourself and do the good inclinations that pour from your loving, kind and gentle heart. You desire to live out this heart expression in an environment of peace, freedom, love, acceptance and affirmation. The wounding crushes this passion.

Where does the wounding come from? It comes from the realities of living life in a world of walking wounded. Normally it begins in childhood. However, it doesn't necessarily have to. It occurs like this:

⇨ *someone does or says something, or*
⇨ *something occurs in your life,*
　➡ *either as a one-time event, or*
　➡ *as a series of occurrences,*
　　➡ *that is emotionally,*
　　　➡ *devastating, painful or traumatic.*

When this happens to you during your childhood, you have thoughts of, *"I wish I could run away."* When it occurs in your teen years or early adult life, you may find yourself attempting anything that will bring relief from the internal emotional pain, feelings and memories (overeating, drug or alcohol abuse, sexual indulgences or extremes, being a workaholic, etc.) When the wounding is severe enough and your other attempts at relief consistently fall short, you may have thoughts as extreme as suicide.

When the wounding enters your heart, it begins the process of an *emotional* metamorphosis or transformation. The *wounded spirit* takes root and produces altered feelings and attitudes within you. These altered feelings and attitudes, in turn, change your mental, emotional, physical and verbal behavior.

### The Shielded Heart

How do you and I normally respond to the wounding?

Frankly, not very well. Usually, because the pain is so intense and painful, we have a tendency to build an encasement, or wall of protection, around our heart. This is our attempt to protect and shield our heart from *further* wounding and pain (see Illus. 8–2).

The problem with this response is that when you erect the encasement or wall, in reality you are *not* shielding your heart from further wounding (though you think or hope you are). You are shielding your heart from being able to feel, experience or receive any legitimate, unconditional *love*. Feelings of love are the *only* things that can genuinely and permanently heal or change

Illus. 8–2: **The Encased Heart**

a wounded heart and set it unconditionally free, *emotionally*. I am personally convinced that this is why the Bible speaks so often of our Creator's love for us.

> *"For God <u>loved</u> the world so much that He gave His only Son; so that anyone who believes in Him shall not perish, but have eternal life."*
>
> *"May your '<u>roots</u>' go down deep into the soil of God's marvelous love; and may you be able to <u>feel</u> and <u>understand</u>, as all God's children should, how long, how wide, how deep, and how high His love really is; and to experience this* **love for** *<u>yourself</u>, though it is so great that you will never see the end of it or fully know and understand it. And at last you will be <u>filled up with God Himself</u>."*
>
> **The Bible**

However, because of the wall of protection that you and I erect, our heart is shielded, and consequently hindered, from receiving its badly needed medicine—unconditional love and acceptance. So when you build the wall or encasement, you convince yourself you are shielding your heart from further wounding. Yet, in actuality, you are imprisoning your heart from being able to receive and experience genuine love, healing, freedom and peace (see Illus. 8–3 on page 106). Consequently, your *emotional*-self, or heart, is destined to remain *imprisoned* by the wounding and pain and all of its subsequent effects.

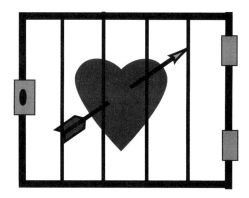

Illus. 8–3: **The Imprisoned Heart**

At this point, because of the realities that accompany the emotional encasement and imprisonment, the wounding further entrenches itself within the heart. It takes "root" *emotionally.* Once wounding is firmly rooted within your heart or *emotional*-self, your *emotional*-self *reacts* to the wounding's presence. Those emotional reactions trigger still more emotional reactions. The *emotional*-self actually experiences a series of emotional reactions or responses, each one being a reaction to the previous one. These reactions to the wounded spirit channel themselves through your *feelings* and *attitudes.* These emotional reactions ultimately consummate as outward emotional behaviors and expressions, or "fruits," such as fear, anger and depression.

In order to have a clearer understanding of this emotional reaction process, again picture your *emotional*-self as a tree (see Illus. 8–1 on page 102). A tree consists of a root, a trunk, branches and fruit. When the wounding enters your heart, the "root" of your *emotional*-self, it seeps in as a poison. This poison alters the "root." Consequently, the altered change progresses up the tree through the trunk and the branches. It ultimately alters and destroys the original fruit—your external behavior. You do not have to fertilize or water this wounded, altered root. It is worse than a weed. It is self-propagating and self-sufficient. So, when left unhealed and left to itself, the wounded spirit produces its own destructive emotional fruit or behavior. That fruit is channeled through feelings and attitudes.

With a tree, the trunk stems from the "root." With the *emotional*-self, the trunk also stems from the "root" (wounded spirit). The feelings, emotions and attitudes within a wounded heart's "trunk" only continue to perpetuate the negative, destructive, downward cycle of emotion and behavior.

What is the fruit of a "wounded spirit"? What kind of emotional reactions, or "trunk," does this destructive emotional "root" produce? We address these questions and probe the emotional "trunk" in depth in the next chapter.

--------- ⬦ ---------

*R e m e m b e r  & R e f l e c t*   1. *An emotional metamorphosis begins within us when wounding enters our lives.*

2. *Wounding, when at the "root" or core of our* **emotional**-*self, produces a "wounded spirit."*

3. *The "wounded spirit," like the roots of a tree, produces a cycled progression of negative and detrimental feelings and attitudes. These feelings and attitudes are* **reactions** *to the pain and wounding. These emotional reactions trigger yet* **additional** *emotions and attitudes, which ultimately consummate as external"fruit," or behavior. All of these feelings and attitudes ultimately become behavioral* **habits**.

# CHAPTER 9

# *What Went Wrong:  The Trunk*
## *Bitterness, Self-Centeredness and Rebellion—*
## *Self-Denial and Compliance*

*I*f wounding is a hell on earth, then what it produces is a life sentence of tormenting fear, pain and anguish.  The *wounded spirit* sets in motion a negative emotional process that ultimately changes what you think, say, feel and do.  Once the *wounded spirit* is rooted and entrenched within your heart, it produces natural "fruits" or emotional *reactions*.  Again, these "fruits" or reactions are feelings and attitudes that spring from the "root" of a wounded spirit within your *emotional*-self.  They are not mental (psychological), physical or spiritual *in nature*.  However, these feelings and attitudes almost always will affect the mental, physical and spiritual areas of your life.

### Bitterness
Once a wounded spirit is firmly rooted within your heart, it produces an emotional reaction or "fruit" of *bitterness* (see Illus. 9–1 on page 110).

*bitterness*

*wounded spirit*

Illus. 9–1: **Bitterness: The Trunk**

When bitterness is produced within your heart you find your-self thinking and feeling things like:

*"Why is this happening to me (the incident that has triggered the wounding—divorce, death, abuse, broken relationship, job loss, unexpected circumstances, etc.)?*

*"This isn't right. It isn't fair.*

*"I don't deserve to be treated this way.*

*"Why are they saying these things about me?*

*"Why are they doing this to me?*

*"Why is God letting this happen to me?"*

The questions and bewilderment go on and on. They mount as no answer brings a satisfying resolution. Feelings of aban-donment, rejection, inferiority and fear grow within your heart. You conclude that you must be the earth's gravel pit. Otherwise, these things surely would not be happening to you, especially as regularly as they do! Invariably, *bitterness* sets in. It firmly plants itself within your heart and mind.

What is bitterness? Bitterness is a *sharp harshness* that develops within your heart and mind. This sharp harshness may be directed toward:

**1**. The person who has most recently wounded, violated or invaded you.

**2**. People, or society in general, especially if your wounding is severe or occurs repeatedly.

**3**. Your Creator. You conclude that He has rejected or abandoned you.

This stands to reason. Because of the wounding, your mind is bombarded with thoughts like:

*"Why did God let this happen to me?"*

When satisfactory answers do not come, you feel a cold, hard slap in your face. It feels similar to what you often feel when your questions are answered with silence by those closest to you. So you conclude that your Creator has given you the same cold shoulder of silence. You may begin thinking:

*"He has rejected me.*

*"He doesn't like me.*

*"I must, in some way, be defective, and therefore, worthy of rejection and the wounding that comes my way.*

*"I can't measure up to God's approval, acceptance or standard."*

So a bitterness toward your Creator sets in.

**4**. Yourself, which is reflected later in life as you struggle with thoughts, words and actions that are very self-condemning and self-destructive.

Bitterness is probably the most destructive of all emotions. The reason for this is clear. Once lodged within your heart, bitterness triggers thoughts, words and deeds that are some of the most destructive and devastating:

> for yourself,
> for your friends and family, and
> for society.

Even the Bible relates warnings about this emotion.

> *"Look after each other so that not one of you will fail to find God's best blessings. Watch out that no <u>bitterness takes root</u> within you, for as it springs up it causes deep trouble, hurting many in their lives."*
>
> **The Bible**

Much of the devastation and destructiveness within our lives, our society, our country and our world can be rooted back to this one emotion. It is obvious that bitterness is something we shouldn't take lightly. Its power is far too destructive. It can run its tentacles through every fiber and facet of our beings—mentally, emotionally, physically and spiritually.

### Self-Centeredness or Self-Denial

Once bitterness has firmly entrenched itself within the heart, our *emotional*-self will react to the feelings of bitterness (much as it reacted to the feelings of the wounding). For most of us the "fruit," or emotional *reaction* to bitterness, is *self-centeredness*. However, for some of us the emotional reaction to bitterness is *self-denial*, which is a direct emotional opposite of self-centeredness (see Illus. 9–2).

When self-centeredness is being manifested or seeded within the heart it triggers thoughts and feelings like this:

> *"Why is this* (the wounding) *happening to me? It's not right or fair. They do not care about me. If they cared for me, they would not be talking to me in this way or treating me in this way. Since they do not care for me, no one does. **Therefore, I have to take care of myself. No one else will. I am going to look after myself for a change. I have always put others first. But not anymore. I am tired of being walked on. I am going to be number one in my life for a while."***

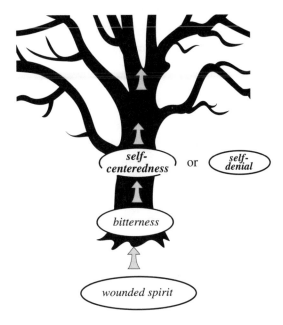

Illus. 9–2: **Self-Centeredness or Self-Denial: The Trunk**

Or this thought process may be directed, not toward the people around you, but toward your Creator:

*"Why is this* (the wounding) *happening to me? Why did God let this happen? It is not right or fair. God does not care about me. If He cared for me, He would not be allowing this to happen. Since God does not care for me, no one does. Therefore, I have to take care of myself. No one else will. I am going to look after myself for a change. I have always put others first, even God. But not anymore. I will be number one in my life for a while."*

For some of us, instead of self-centeredness, we react to bitterness with self-denial. Self-denial is a discounting or deprivation of one's self and heart-nature. Because of the wounding, you conclude that the violator must be right in their violation or assessment of you. Therefore, you discount and deny your own value, worth or personhood. Consequently, you do not and will not stand up for, or affirm, your own value, worth or personhood. When self-denial is the reaction within your *emotional*-self it causes you to think things like this:

*"They (the offender or violator) must be right and I must be wrong. Why else would they do or say these things to me?"*

Because of this thought process (of self-centeredness and self-denial), we lead ourselves into a mode of self-preservation and self-protection. Ultimately, a fear-based life style develops. In a very unhealthy manner, we become preoccupied with ourselves. We feel we must stand guard over our emotions, making sure nothing and no one will intrude and bring further wounding and pain. (Remember the encased and imprisoned hearts in Chapter Eight).

The problem with this attitude is that we ignorantly destroy and sabotage many, if not most, of the good and pleasurable relationships, activities and pleasures that come into our lives. We sabotage them because we fear they may wound, harm and bring additional pain into our lives. Ultimately, because of the fear, we ignorantly destroy the relationship, job, activity or pleasure before it has a chance to destroy or wound us.

When self-centeredness or self-denial seeds within us, we develop an entire life style around it. We nurture it. We accommodate it. Why? Because we become convinced that accomodating the self-centeredness or self-denial will be our only hope for emotional protection and preservation—or so we feel and believe.

### Self-Centeredness vs. Self-Affirmed Living

This is not to say that you should deny your heart nature. No. In order to live life in love, healing, freedom and peace, you must live a healthy life style of *knowing who you are in your heart-nature.* You must develop a life style that *accommodates* your heart-nature in every area of your life. This requires a healthy, *self-affirming* approach to life and living. There are two main differences between a healthy *self-affirming* life style and an un-healthy *self-centeredness:*

**1.** *Self-centeredness* is spawned from self-protection and self-preservation. Self-protection and self-preservation are triggered by fear, wounding and emotional pain.

*Self-affirmed* living stems from the healthy, objective real-ization that you and I are unique in heart, nature, character and identity. Therefore, we each need to be sure that every relation-ship, job, venture and activity in our lives genuinely "fits" our specific heart-nature. All too often we overlook this reality and attempt to *force-fit* ourselves into relationships, jobs and activi-ties that do not fit our heart-nature, thereby setting off negative and detrimental consequences for ourselves.

**2.** Since it comes from wounding, *self-centeredness* pro-duces a self-imposed imprisonment for the person living within its borders. You hope it provides freedom from pain, wounding and fear. It does not. It steals your freedom. You lose the free-dom to live, breathe and be yourself in all environments and around all types of people. You find yourself *performing* in hopes of "fitting in" and being accepted.

*Self-affirmed* living produces freedom. By seeing to it that your outward environment accommodates and fits with your heart-nature, you subsequently feel the freedom to be yourself and express yourself—freely, without fear of rejection, hurt, wound-ing or pain.

You will know you are healed and free when you feel relaxed enough to be able to freely express yourself and be yourself in the environment around you. *That* is *self-affirmed* living; it is not *self-centeredness.*

**Rebellion or Compliance**

Once self-centeredness has been firmly seeded or entrenched within your heart or *emotional*-self, it too, will trigger an emo-tional reaction or produce a natural emotional fruit. For most of us, the emotional fruit of self-centeredness is *rebellion.*

However when the previous reaction has been self-denial, *compliance* almost always follows (see Illus. 9–3).

When you and I hear the word "rebellion" we usually think of things like the riots of the sixties or now, even the nineties. Riots are the rawest form of aggressive, demonstrative defiance and rebellion.

However, the emotional process that leads to and produces feelings and attitudes of rebellion is not necessarily demonstrated as outward, aggressive defiance. Usually, the emotional rebellion we are referring to here is much more quiet, hidden and subtle. Only in its extreme form will it manifest itself in outward aggression.

Emotional rebellion is a feeling and attitude of *resistance*. This type of rebellion is *defensive* in nature. It is not offensive or aggressive in nature. It is a defensive rebellion, a rebellion for defensive, protective purposes. The picture of this type of rebel-

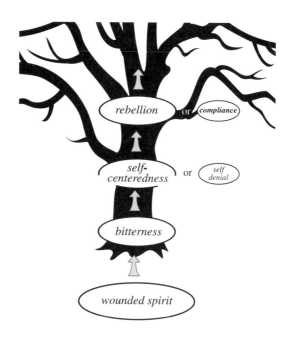

Illus. 9–3: **Rebellion or Compliance:  The Trunk**

lion is that of a wounded person pushing away all attempts by others to help assist, lead, direct, guide or influence his or her life. It is a picture of one keeping everything and everyone at arm's length, even to the degree of resisting, defying and rebelling against authority or those around him or her. This type of rebellion is more of a resistance than a defiance. Outwardly, though, it looks the same as the outward, defiant rebellion. Those around it usually can not differentiate between the two.

The resistance may initially be innocent, motivated out of a desire to protect yourself from further pain and wounding. However, its end consequence is always a destructive death to the whole, non-wounded *emotional*-self—the *real*-self that was you before any wounding or pain ever entered your heart.

Interestingly enough, for some of us, we react to the self-centeredness or self-denial with an emotion opposite to rebellion—*compliance*.

Compliance is an emotional passiveness that causes you to appease and please others, usually at the expense of your own heart-nature and personal identity. With compliance, you take on an emotional behavior that attempts to keep life calm—you will do anything to keep from rocking the boat and risking another's disapproval, scorn or rejection. Like self denial, this emotional reaction occurs less frequently than its counterpart—rebellion. However, it has the same negative life-altering effect on your life and personality.

As a way of review, once seeded within your heart, wounding triggers thoughts and feelings such as those in Illus. 9–4 on page 118. Begin reading the illustration from the *bottom* to the top, starting with the *wounded spirit.*

At this point, it is important to remember that the process we are referring to is *emotional*. It is not physical, mental or spiritual. So, we can now begin to see how this negative emotional process would affect our mental, physical and spiritual areas of living. The power and reality of our *emotional*-self is incredible, isn't it?

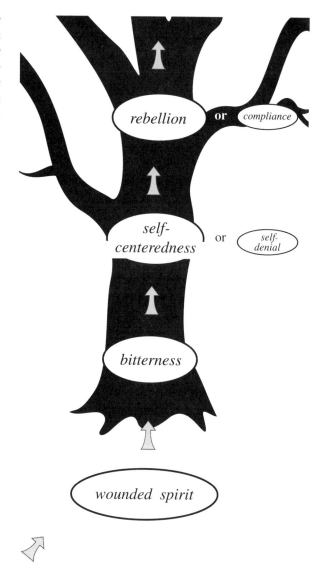

*"I don't give a flip about them or what they want or need. Why should I? Look at what they think about me (the wounding)."*

*"They don't care for me, so I'll look out for myself."*

*"Why am I being treated or talked to this way. It's not right or fair."*

*"Why did this happen to me (the wounding)?"*

(starting here)

Illus. 9–4: **The Wounded *Emotional*-Self: The Trunk**

So, initially, this wounded transformation and change may seem innocent, but once entrenched within the heart, it sets off a cycle of events that develops into a destructive *habit* life style. We will look in detail at the effects both rebellion and compliance have on our heart, mind and life in the next chapter.

————— ⚐ —————

*Remember & Reflect*

**1.** *A **wounded spirit** produces feelings and attitudes of **bitterness**.*

**2.** ***Bitterness** produces feelings and attitudes of **self-centeredness** (or **self-denial**).*

**3.** ***Self-centeredness** produces feelings and attitudes of **rebellion** (or **compliance**).*

**4.** *This process is **emotional**, not physical, mental or spiritual, in nature. However, it almost always will affect the mental, physical and spiritual areas of our lives. It is an **emotional** process that takes over and controls our feelings and attitudes. When these feelings and attitudes are felt and experienced often enough, they eventually become behavioral **habits**.*

# CHAPTER 10

# *The Mystery Revealed:  Three Fruits*
## *Our Wounded Outward Behavior*

*O*nce feelings, emotions and attitudes of emotional rebellion (or compliance) are firmly entrenched within the heart, what happens next?  What course, or path, do your feelings and emotions take?  Once again, we can find the answers to these questions in the Bible.

In a section of the Bible titled Jude, a verse says,

> *"Yet in the same manner these men, also by dreaming, <u>defile the flesh</u>, and <u>reject authority</u>, and <u>revile angelic majesties</u>."*
>
> **The Bible**

The first part of this sentence refers to people who are extremely off balance.  The last part of the sentence, the description of their imbalance, is what is significant.  The latter portion of the sentence refers to three distinct, externally manifested behaviors that are exhibited by these  people:

> *defiling the flesh,*
> *rejecting authority* and
> *reviling angelic majesties.*

121

As we read these words we can see that there is a significance, but what is it? Why are these three terms mentioned? Why not some other words or phrases? Why these particular phrases, and why is it *three* phrases? Not one, or two, or four, or five, but three? There is a significance, but what is it?

The significance is twofold. First, these three phrases refer to external *outward behaviors,* or *"fruits."* Remember the emotional tree (our *emotional*-self) that bears outward, emotional "fruit" or behavior?

The second issue of significance is that these three groupings of externally manifested behaviors reveal the three avenues or *"branches"* through which our wounding and pain propels itself within our *emotional*-self.

### Three Realms of Relationship

The three basic realms of *relationship* in our lives are:
> relationship with *ourselves,*
> relationship with *those around us* and
> relationship with *our Creator* and the *spirit realm.*

There are *three*, and only three, avenues or *branches* through which our feelings and emotions channel themselves. Therefore, for the wounded-self, emotional rebellion (or compliance) will manifest itself *through these three distinct channels.* These three *branches* are related to, and connected with, the three realms of relationship in each of our lives: relationship with our self, others, and our Creator. Once through these three channels, wounding, transformed into the stage of rebellion (or compliance), will manifest itself through outward behaviors that:
> *defile the flesh,*
> *reject authority* and
> *revile angelic majesties* (see Illus. 10–1).

We will explore these three *"branches"* in detail in Chapters Ten, Eleven, and Twelve. However, before doing that, let's take a closer look at the three fruits—the final destination of the wounding process—our wounded outward behavior.

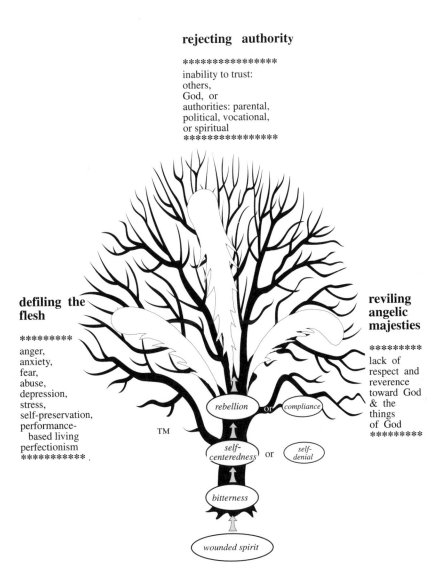

rejecting authority

****************
inability to trust:
others,
God, or
authorities: parental,
political, vocational,
or spiritual
****************

defiling the
flesh

*********
anger,
anxiety,
fear,
abuse,
depression,
stress,
self-preservation,
performance-
  based living
perfectionism
***********

reviling
angelic
majesties

*********
lack of
respect and
reverence
toward God
& the
things
of God
*********

rebellion  or  compliance

self-
centeredness  or  self-
denial

bitterness

wounded spirit

Illus. 10–1: **The Three Emotional "Fruits" of a Wounded Spirit**

### Defiling the Flesh

What does this mean? The word "flesh" indicates that the intended meaning of this phrase is *personal*. It is something self-contained within an individual. It obviously pertains to some type of self-destructive behavior.

The word "defile" means to destroy the pureness and cleanness of something, to make dirty. This is what wounding does to our hearts. It causes us to take on a behavior that tarnishes our hearts. The altered behavior makes us do, say and think things that cause us to give up and lose our felt sense of emotional purity, cleanness and wholeness.

Specifically, defiling the flesh is anything (actions, words, feelings or thoughts) that slowly, like a cancer, can eat away at and eventually destroy some aspect of our human entity or existence—either mentally, emotionally, physically or spiritually.

This includes emotions and behavior such as anger, anxiety, abuse, fear, depression, perfectionism, performance-based living and compulsive behavior.

These things, when left to influence and control our thinking, feelings and actions, will eventually, like a cancer, destroy some aspect of our human existence—our mental, emotional, physical or even spiritual existence.

### Rejecting Authority

This refers to our interaction, feelings and attitude toward authorities in our lives. However, when the wounding is severe enough, it will not limit itself to the authorities in our lives. It will manifest itself in *all* of our relationships—relations with family, friends, peers, etc.

In its rawest, purest form, *rejecting authority* is an emotion that cuts off our ability to trust others. It renders us incapable of trusting others for fear of further wounding by those in whom we would trust. This stands to reason. Because of the past wounding, especially by those in whom we had placed our trust, we find it very difficult to be able to relaxingly trust and wait on others.

**Reviling Angelic Majesties**

This phrase refers to our interaction, feelings and attitudes toward angels, the spiritual world and our Creator.

It is a mocking or slandering toward your Creator or the spirit realm. It usually exists because of deep pain and wounding we feel toward our Creator. It triggers when something occurrs in our lives that is emotionally painful and we feel that God let us down. Many unresolved questions arise and it eventually became easier to question the existence of a Creator than to try and reconcile our confused, painful and unanswered questions with regard to our Creator's interaction or intervention in our lives.

What does all of this mean? How does it relate to you or me and our wounding and pain? The answers surface in the following chapters as we follow the *"branches"* that our wounded emotions take from the trunk (rebellion /compliance), up to the outward "fruit" (the three behaviors mentioned above).

------- ◊ -------

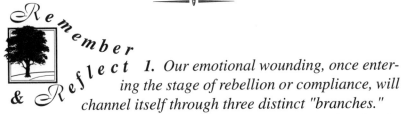

*1. Our emotional wounding, once entering the stage of rebellion or compliance, will channel itself through three distinct "branches."*

*2. The three branches are related to and connected with the three basic realms of relationship in our lives.*

*3. Once through the branches, our wounding and pain will ultimately conclude its journey by thrusting itself out of our being through three distinct aspects of outward behavior, or "fruits."*

*4. The three distinct, outward "fruits" are:*
    *defiling the flesh*
    *rejecting authority and*
    *reviling angelic majesties.*

# CHAPTER 11

# *A Lack of Responsibility:*
# *The First Branch*
## *The Wounded-Self*

 From the position of rebel-
lion (or compliance), emotional wounding develops into and
through three specific channels or "branches":

A Lack of Responsibility,
A Lack of Respect and
A Lack of Reverence.

These three "branches" are each related to and are connected
with the three realms of relationship in our lives:

relationship with our self,
relationship with others and
relationship with our Creator and the spirit realm.

### A Lack of Responsibility

The first branch through which emotional rebellion and compliance both often channel themselves is through "A Lack of
Responsibility" (see Illus. 11–1). This branch affects your rela-

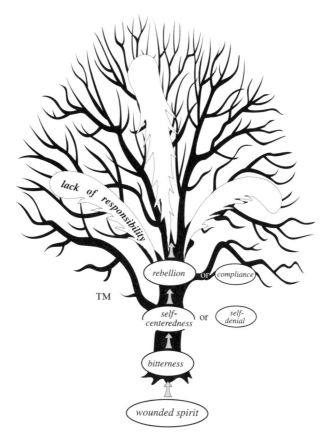

Illus. 11–1: **A Lack of Responsibility:  The First Branch**

tionship with yourself and produces emotional outward behavior, or "fruit", that "defiles the flesh".

When most of us hear "a lack of responsibility"  we react with,

> *"That is not me.  I take care of my responsibilities.  I work.  I pay my bills.  I take care of those under my care."*

However, what we are speaking of here is not that kind of responsibility.  We are not referring to physical responsibility. Most of us, by nature, are very responsible with the physical aspect of our lives.

Remember, this negative transforming process that takes place within you and me is *emotional.* It is not physical, spiritual or mental. Because this process is emotional, it is usually very difficult to recognize. In their infancy, feelings and attitudes of emotional irresponsibility are hard to detect. In fact, most of us are not aware of their presence until after we have had to live with the effects they have brought upon us for quite some time, maybe even years. Even then, most of us have a difficult time connecting the outward *fruit,* or outwardly displayed behavior, with the inward branch—a lack of personal responsibility, or emotional irresponsibility.

With this in mind, let's see how you can know when "a lack of responsibility" is a factor within your *emotional*-self, and consequently, your life style.

Unknowingly and subconsciously, you will find yourself looking to other people and situations to gain a sense of who you are. Additionally, you will also find yourself hoping in the situations and circumstances surrounding your life to gain your sense of how you feel. Or, you will blame other people or external events for the circumstances surrounding your life. This is rather important, so let's look at it again.

"A lack of personal responsibility," or *emotional irresponsibility,* is a part of my life when I find myself:

> *looking to,*
> *blaming,*
> *holding responsible, or*
> *hoping in*
>> *other people,*
>> *situations, or*
>> *circumstances outside of myself*
>> *to gain my sense of:*
>>> *who I am,*
>>> *how I feel, or*
>>> *for the circumstances*
>>> *surrounding my life."*

We do this effortlessly. It happens when we look to a boss or mate to affirm us. It happens when we hope that a particular job will feed us our sense of identity and purpose. It is a trap, one that is easy to fall into.

### Emotional Saviors

Having experienced what we have through our counseling services, I would speculate that as much as *eighty percent* of humanity either currently practices or has in the past practiced a life style or approach to living that flows through this "branch" of emotional irresponsibility. It is a natural effect or "fruit" of a *wounded spirit.*

It is an approach to life where you look to someone outside of yourself to satisfy or fulfill every emotional aspect of your life. Unknowingly, you are looking for an *emotional savior*— someone to complete your life (remember Chapter Six). You are looking for that certain someone who will nurture you, guide you, guard you, protect you and lead you through the treacheries of society and life. You are looking for safety. You are looking for direction. You are looking for the answers to some of life's most challenging questions (questions about yourself and your life's purpose). You are looking for someone to help you feel good about you—an emotional savior. Approaching life and relationships in this way causes major problems, which, in turn, trigger major emotional imbalances.

### Returning To The Womb

Out of fear, hurt and pain, we naturally want to "return to the womb." The womb is warm, safe and secure. However, in reality, we know it is impossible to return to the womb. But, we try to anyway—emotionally. So, without realizing it, we attempt to experience the same *emotional* benefits we experienced when in the safety and security of the womb by looking to or hoping in someone outside of ourselves for our own peace, love, joy, stability and fulfillment. We seek an emotional savior.

When these "saviors" let us down, we feel hurt, wounded, abandoned and betrayed. When they don't perform to our hopes and expectations, our lives remain unfulfilled. We then take those very same people we were hoping in and looking to, the emotional saviors, and we blame them or hold them responsible for the negative feelings or the problems surrounding our lives. Do you see how we do this?

At this point, the emotional cycle or process takes it's most devastating turn. Why? Because if we are looking to, hoping in or blaming someone else for who we are, how we feel or for the circumstances surrounding our lives, *we have given up control of our emotional life.* We have, in turn, placed that control on the external person or influence in which we are hoping. We are no longer in control of our lives or emotions because we gave the control to the one whom we began looking to, hoping in or holding responsible. What is the significance of this? What's so bad about losing control or giving up control of your life and emotional well-being, in hopes of being taken care of emotionally? Plenty!

### Depression and Depressive Behavior

When you give up emotional control to influences outside of yourself, at that point you enter the threshold of depression and depressive behavior. When it is inside you, depression triggers feelings that make you think things such as:

> *"I have no control or say-so with my life or with my own feelings. Others have more control and more of a say-so with my feelings than I do. I am powerless. Others are in control of my feelings. I am not."*

Thoughts and feelings of hopelessness, defeat, no control and no say-so establish themselves as constant companions at this point in your life.

These are the thoughts and feelings with which depression blasts its recipients. From this stage you enter an even deeper negative cycle. You lose mental and physical motivation to live.

This stands to reason.  Why would people want to live if they could not have a determination in their own lives and feelings? Who wants to live a life where everyone else has more control or say-so over them and their feelings than they do themselves? What is there to live for?

In its extreme form, depressive behavior will even manifest itself by causing the individual to ball up into a fetal position or live for days in bed.  The feeling is:

> *"Why should I get up and live life?  Nothing is going to change.  I am not in control of it.  Everyone else, including God, has the control over my life and feelings.  I have nothing to live for.*
>
> *"I'll just stay here, where it is safe.*
>
> *This way I will not have to make any decisions and if I don't have to make any decisions I will not have to worry about making a mistake."*

How does this happen?  How is it that *not* exercising personal, emotional control  leads to depression?  Well, it makes very good sense when you think about it.

> *"I gave up the control of my life and my emotions when I began looking to you, or hoping in you, or holding you responsible for my sense of who I am, how I feel or for the circumstances surrounding my life.*
>
> *"I began looking to you, holding you responsible or hoping in you to **do**, **be** or **perform** in such a way that would cause me to feel good about my life, my environment, my circumstances or myself.*
>
> *"When I began looking to you, I held a hope that you would take control **for** me and provide me with happiness, love, peace and fulfillment.*
>
> *"So, when I began to place my hope in you to control my life and happiness for me, **I relinquished control**, emotionally."*

This happens to millions of us. It is not a conscious thought process, though. It is emotional. We do it subconsciously. We do it without even thinking about it.

At this point, depressive behavior—the feeling of absolute powerlessness over your life and feelings—can trigger major mental imbalances. It can also trigger physical chemical imbalances within your system as well. However, the depressive behavior and the imbalances can be conquered and cured.

The important thing to realize here is that all of this pain and all of these problems were first triggered by feelings and attitudes that caused you to give over control of your internal self, your mental self *and* your *emotional*-self, to other people, forces or influences outside of yourself. At the time, you probably were not aware that you were relinquishing control of your life. No one ever is. You surely were not aware of the devastating effects this decision would have on your life and feelings.

Our Creator created you and me in such a way that demands that we each exercise control, leadership and direction over our entire being:  mentally, emotionally, spiritually and physically. When this is not occurring, for whatever reason—usually because of our reactions to wounding, fear and pain—it causes emotional imbalances (such as fear, anger and depression.) Because of the power and influence that the *emotional*-self has over the rest of our beings, the emotional imbalances then trigger additional imbalances within our mental, physical and spiritual lives as well.

### Defiling the Flesh

Once you are in a position of *not* exercising personal emotional responsibility (a lack of responsibility), the emotionally irresponsible feelings and attitudes will project themselves outwardly from your being in the form of mental *thoughts*, emotional *feelings*, physical *actions* and verbal *words and phrases*. They will produce outward "fruit" or *behavior* that "defiles the flesh" (Chapter Ten). It is this outward "fruit" or behavior that you and everyone around you will witness. What type of fruit or outward behavior does emotional irresponsibility—a lack of personal responsibility—produce?

anger
anxiety
fear of man
fear of failure
fear of rejection
fear of inadequacy
fear of abandonment
verbal abuse
sexual abuse
physical abuse
substance abuse
alcohol abuse
eating disorders
depression
stress
self-preservation
self-protection
performance-based living
perfectionism
and much more

These and other outwardly manifested "fruits" or behaviors, when left unattended, will, after repetition, become *habit*—mentally, emotionally, verbally and physically.  Eventually, these *habits* become an active part of your life style.  At that point, you feel very much out of control.  You have not been able to do anything to stop or break these behaviors from your life, not permanently, anyway.  After years of living with these habits, you grow accustomed to them.  They become familiar acquaintances.  You even begin believing that they are an actual part of your heart-nature, personality or character.

It is at this point that your life is producing "fruit" or behavior that *"defiles the flesh"* (see Ilus. 11–2).

Remember from the previous chapter that the definition for "defiling the flesh" is:

> *Anything that slowly, like a cancer, can eat away at and eventually destroy some aspect of your existence (either mentally, emotionally, physically or spiritually).*

When your *emotional*-self is left unhealed, and the negative, detrimental fruits are left to rule and have control over you and

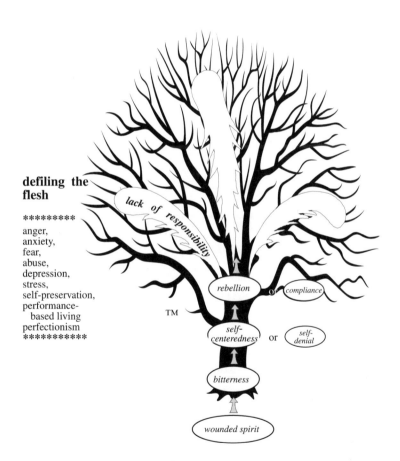

Illus. 11–2: **Defiling the Flesh: the Fruit**

your life, these negative, wounded fruits—such as fear, anger and depression—will, like a cancer, slowly eat away at your life. They will slowly eat away at you and eventually destroy some aspect of your existence—mentally, physically, emotionally or even spiritually.

Now, as you look back over the emotional path (the tree) that your wounding and pain takes, a path that begins with a "root" of a *wounded spirit*, you can now see how the wounding runs its course and ultimately changes your behavior (what you *feel*, what you *think*, what you *say* and what you *do*), can't you? It is a changed behavior that will inevitably destroy the *real* you, either mentally, emotionally, physically or spiritually.

However, there is more. Emotional rebellion and/or compliance not only manifests itself through the "branch" of "A Lack of Responsibility"; it also channels its energies through two additional "branches." We explore the next "branch" in the following chapter.

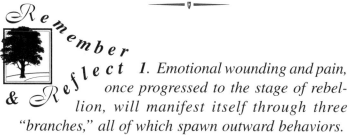

*1. Emotional wounding and pain, once progressed to the stage of rebellion, will manifest itself through three "branches," all of which spawn outward behaviors.*

*2. The first "branch" is "A Lack of Responsibility," personally.*

*3. This emotionally irresponsible approach to life will often lead to fear, anger or depression.*

*4. This "branch" of emotional irresponsibility always produces outward behaviors or "fruits" that, when left to themselves, uncontrolled, will "defile the flesh"; that is they will destroy the **real** you either mentally, physically, emotionally or spiritually.*

*5. This "fruit" is directed toward yourself.*

# CHAPTER 12

# *A Lack of Respect:*
# *The Second Branch*
## *The Wounded-Self*

$\mathcal{T}$he second branch through which emotional rebellion, or compliance, will channel themselves is "A Lack of Respect" (see Illus. 12–1). This branch affects your relationship with others and produces the fruit of "rejecting authority".

### A Lack of Respect

What is "a lack of respect"? It is more than what most of us initially think it is. It is more than just a matter of respect or disrespect toward others. Because of this, it too, is very difficult to recognize. So then, how can we detect its presence in our lives? Here's how. When "a lack of respect" is resident within your heart it feels something like this:

> *"Deep within myself, I find myself having a difficult time being able to totally, whole-heartedly **trust** other people, especially those who are a close part of my life."*

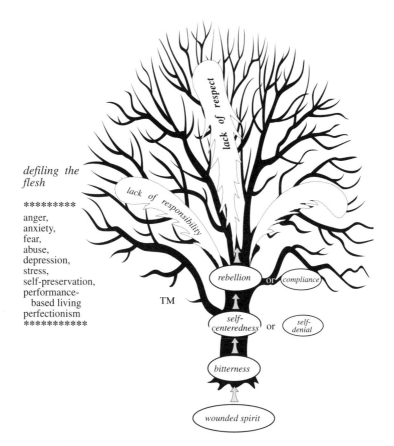

*defiling the flesh*

*********
anger,
anxiety,
fear,
abuse,
depression,
stress,
self-preservation,
performance-
  based living
perfectionism
**********

Illus. 12–1: **A Lack of Respect: The Branch**

This usually pertains to the authorities in our lives. There are four basic areas of authority: political, vocational, parental and spiritual. However, if or when the wounding in our lives has been extremely severe, we will find that we not only have difficulty trusting authority, but we also find it hard to trust other people in general, whether they are in authority over us or not.

Why is this so? Well, it stands to reason. Especially, when seen in light of emotional wounding and pain. It causes us to feel something like this:

*"Look at the wounding and pain I have had to endure (the "root" or wounded spirit). That occurred when I had no choice but to trust.*

*"So now, you want me to trust again? You have to be kidding. I do not intend to set myself up for that type of hurt and pain again. There is no way I am ever going to be that vulnerable again!"*

So we develop a life style of self-preservation and protection. It is unthinkable to consider trusting others. Why? Because we can't afford to let down our guard and risk being hurt again. The pain is far too intense.

Consequently, we continue through life always projecting a facade of trust, but never really trusting. We tell others we trust them, but deep within ourselves, we feel we can't really afford to trust. We will ask someone to do their part. However, we are always having to look over their shoulder, or call and touch base, just to make sure they are going to keep their end of the bargain.

Why are we doing this? Because when we are in a position of unconditional trust or reliance with someone outside of ourselves, a forceful *knot* starts to build within us. Sometimes it is so strong that it feels as though it will explode within us. That knot is a *fear* of being hurt, let down or wounded again.

Eventually, our real attitude (of mistrust) reveals itself. This, in turn, causes major relational and emotional conflicts with others in our life. Why? Because they feel hurt, wounded and rejected by us and our mistrust. They feel that our mistrust of them is because we believe there is a flaw in them, not in us. So, they react. Out of pain and wounding, they react. Eventually, the relationship goes sour.

### Unhealthy, Destructive Control

When we experience this "branch" as a regular part of our life style, we will always try to exercise or exert control in everything we do and with those we are around. This is an unhealthy control. It is a negative controlling behavior that causes us to try to dictate and control everything and everyone in our external lives. We do this as an attempt to control our internal lives—our feelings and fears. However, it never works. It only destroys.

Additionally, this type of external control is different from the healthy, internal control we first spoke of in Chapter Six. We will explore that healthy type of control in more detail in "Part III: The Other Side of Life."

### Rejecting Authority

The inability to trust others will always manifest itself through the outward "fruit" of "rejecting authority" as discussed in Chapter Ten (see Illus. 12–2).

This "fruit" is just what it says it is.
⇨ *You **reject** because you don't trust.*
➡ *You **don't trust** out of fear and risk of being hurt and wounded again.*
➡ *You **fear** being hurt and wounded again.*

Why? Because you are all too familiar with the devastating consequences of the initial wounding and pain you first encountered years earlier (your "wounded spirit" experiences).

So you see, because of the past wounding and pain, and the emotional progression or metamorphosis and change which our *emotional*-self goes through, many of us develop an approach to life, living and relationships that "rejects authority." Remember, this is not physical, mental or spiritual. It is *emotional*. It is feelings and attitudes. However, because it is emotional, it will almost always affect the mental, physical and spiritual aspects of our lives.

This rejection of authority may be manifested outwardly, in the form of overt defiance. More often, however, it is very quiet, hidden and subtle. Because it is *emotional* (feelings and attitudes), it is *internal*. You work hard to keep it internal. However, it is an attitude and feeling. So, no matter how hard you try to keep it quiet, this *"lack of respect"* or inability to trust, will always show itself and manifest its presence through outward

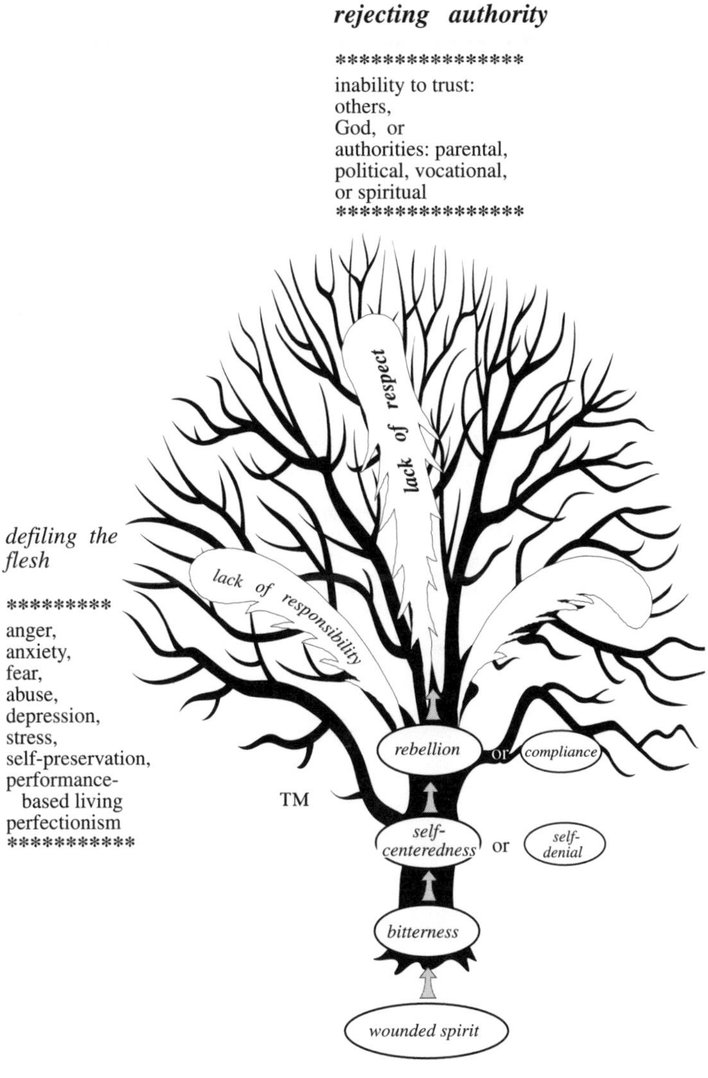

*rejecting  authority*

\*\*\*\*\*\*\*\*\*\*\*\*\*\*\*\*
inability to trust:
others,
God,  or
authorities: parental,
political, vocational,
or spiritual
\*\*\*\*\*\*\*\*\*\*\*\*\*\*\*\*

lack of respect

*defiling  the*
*flesh*

\*\*\*\*\*\*\*\*\*
anger,
anxiety,
fear,
abuse,
depression,
stress,
self-preservation,
performance-
  based living
perfectionism
\*\*\*\*\*\*\*\*\*\*\*

*lack of responsibility*

*rebellion*  or  *compliance*

TM

*self-centeredness*  or  *self-denial*

*bitterness*

*wounded spirit*

Illus.  12–2:  **Rejecting Authority:  The Fruit**

fruit that *"rejects authority."* Once exposed, it inevitably ruins and destroys your friendships and relationships.

Not only will emotional rebellion and/or compliance produce *a lack of responsibility* (which is directed toward yourself) and *a lack of respect* (which is directed toward your relationship with others around you), but rebellion and/or compliance also channels its energy through a third "branch." We will explore this third "branch" in the next chapter.

———— ❡ ————

*Remember & Reflect*   *1. The second "branch" is "A Lack of respect," toward others.*

*2. This "lack of respect" approach to life exists because of an inability to **trust** others.*

*3. This inability to trust others produces a "fruit" of "rejection of authority."*

*4. When left unbridled and uncontrolled, this emotional "fruit" inevitably ruins and destroys your friendships and relationships.*

# CHAPTER 13

# A Lack of Reverence:
# The Third Branch
## The Wounded-Self

*T*he third and final branch through which rebellion or compliance will channel themselves is "A Lack of Reverence." This branch affects your relationship with your Creator and the spirit realm (see Illus. 13–1). It produces the fruit of "reviling angelic majesties."

### A Lack of Reverence

What is "reverence"? It is a *feeling* and *attitude* of deep *respect* and *honor*, with a sense of *wonder*, *love* and *devotion* toward your Creator and the ways of your Creator. As with the two previously discussed emotional "branches," a lack of reverence is also sometimes difficult to recognize. So how can we know if "a lack of reverence" is a part of our lives? By recognizing how it *feels* within us. Here's how it may feel:

> *"Unknowingly and subconsciously, I find myself having a deeply seeded hurt or pain toward my Creator or His ways in life."*

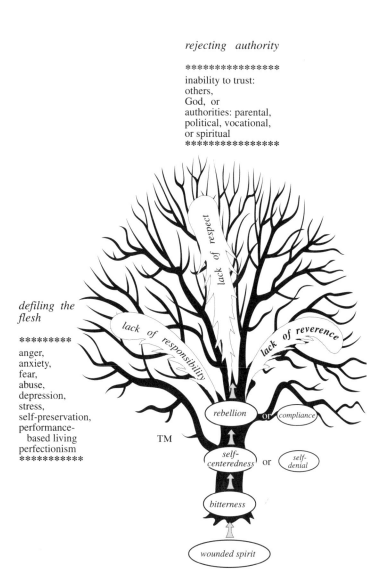

*rejecting   authority*

\*\*\*\*\*\*\*\*\*\*\*\*\*\*\*\*
inability to trust:
others,
God,  or
authorities: parental,
political, vocational,
or spiritual
\*\*\*\*\*\*\*\*\*\*\*\*\*\*\*\*

*lack of respect*

*defiling the flesh*

\*\*\*\*\*\*\*\*\*
anger,
anxiety,
fear,
abuse,
depression,
stress,
self-preservation,
performance-
    based living
perfectionism
\*\*\*\*\*\*\*\*\*\*

*lack of responsibility*

*lack of reverence*

*rebellion*   or  *compliance*

TM

*self-centeredness*   or   *self-denial*

*bitterness*

*wounded spirit*

Illus.  13–1:  **A Lack of Reverence:  The Third Branch**

Why? Because we feel, as a result of the wounding, as if our Creator let us down. The thoughts within us run something like this:

> *"Well, if God is who He says He is, and if He can do the works and miracles He says He can do, and if He loves me as much has He says He does, why did He let the wounding and pain enter my life in the first place? At the time I needed Him the most, where was He? He abandoned me, rejected me and let me down. Maybe He let this happen to me because I am not good enough for Him, life or society. Or maybe He let this happen because He is not really there after all. Maybe He really does not even exist. It would surely explain why He wasn't there when I needed Him the most."*

At this point you end up having a lot more questions than you have answers. You also have a lot more pain. So the easiest thing to do is to attempt to sever your Creator from your life. This is the same mechanism most of us turn to when emotional pain connects with a human relationship; we cut off the human relationship. It seems to be the easiest way to cope with the negative feelings and pain that always accompany thoughts and memories of the relationship. Eventually, a distancing and disconnection occurs within your heart and life style toward the Creator who birthed you and blessed you into His image. After years of this, you become much more aware of the feelings of disconnection than you do of the severing of the emotional cord between you and your Creator. You realize an emotional void exists. You have lost your sense of *connection*, emotionally.

As a matter of fact, once in this state of being, most of us never do make the mental connection that our lost sense of *emotional connection*, emotionally, is directly linked to, and a consequence of, our abandonment of the *connection* we once pursued between our Creator and ourselves. Consequently, we develop a life style that attempts to acquire this missing feeling of *connection* through other avenues. Invariably, our attempts center on the earthly, tangible relationships, activities and vocational opportunities surrounding us. We work like ants to gain a sense of *connection* through the tangible things and relationships around us. For the most part though, these pursuits do not fully satisfy. They can't. They are not supposed to fill that emotional need for *connection* within our lives. The tangibles are meant to *enhance* an already "connected" life style, not fulfill it. That is a function reserved for our Creator.

This "lack of reverence" toward God and the things of God is not to be confused with "a lack of respect" toward the people of God. Often, many of us do correlate the two. Because of some hurt or wound brought on us by the blindness, ignorance or even selfishness of someone or some group representing God, we sometimes vent and direct our unresolved hurt or anger toward God. This then can also create *a lack of respect* toward God. However, it is a misguided decision. Why would you let your feelings and reactions toward other people sever a very valuable and needed emotional relationship in your life? Many of us do, but only to our own harm or demise.

### Reviling Angelic Majesties

Once "a lack of reverence" is a part of our *emotional*-self, it will manifest itself outward from our beings through the fruit of "reviling angelic majesties" (see Illus 13:2). In its lesser form, this is a lack of respect or honor toward our Creator and His ways in life. (It is not to be confused with a lack of respect toward those representing or following their God). In its severest form, this is an aggressive mocking, disrespect and irreverence toward one's Creator and His ways. This extreme display usually surfaces because of intense anger toward one's Creator and His ways. It is what the Bible refers to as blasphemy. Etymologically, the word "revile" means "blasphemous." Acccording to *The World Book Dictionary*, the word blasphemy means, "Abuse of, cursing, reviling or contempt for God or sacred things."

It is important to note that when we are following this "branch," we have to consciously reject our own *natural* desires and inclinations of pursuing, being close to and feeling connected

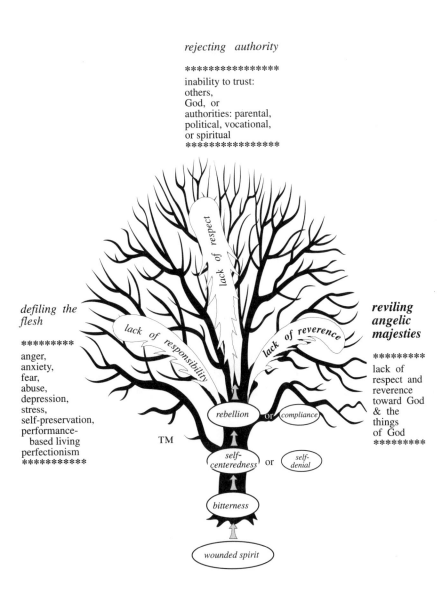

*rejecting   authority*

\*\*\*\*\*\*\*\*\*\*\*\*\*\*\*\*
inability to trust:
others,
God,  or
authorities: parental,
political, vocational,
or spiritual
\*\*\*\*\*\*\*\*\*\*\*\*\*\*\*\*

*lack  of  respect*

*defiling  the
flesh*

\*\*\*\*\*\*\*\*\*
anger,
anxiety,
fear,
abuse,
depression,
stress,
self-preservation,
performance-
 based living
perfectionism
\*\*\*\*\*\*\*\*\*\*\*

*lack  of  responsibility*

*lack  of  reverence*

*reviling
angelic
majesties*

\*\*\*\*\*\*\*\*\*
lack  of
respect and
reverence
toward God
& the
things
of God
\*\*\*\*\*\*\*\*\*

*rebellion*  or  *compliance*

TM

*self-
centeredness*  or  *self-
denial*

*bitterness*

*wounded spirit*

**Illus.  13–2:  Reviling Angelic Majesties:  The Fruit**

with, our Creator. Willfully rejecting this natural inward inclination always causes additional major internal conflict and turmoil. Consequently, this inner turmoil triggers even more anger and pain. This is usually outwardly evident to those around us. In other words, to carry on this behavior, we must "war and battle" against our own internal heart nature which desires to feel *connected* with our Creator. This, in turn, causes yet more anger, rage and pain.

———— ɑ ————

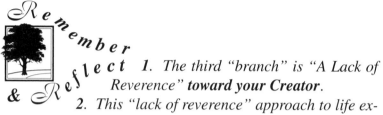

*Remember & Reflect*

1. *The third "branch" is "A Lack of Reverence" **toward your Creator.***

2. *This "lack of reverence" approach to life exists because of a lack of respect toward your Creator and His ways.*

3. *This inability to respect and revere your Creator, produces a fruit of "reviling (mocking) angelic majesties (spirit realm)."*

4. *When left unbridled and uncontrolled, this emotional "fruit" inevitably ruins and destroys your relationship and felt "**connection**" with your Creator.*

5. *This third "fruit" or emotional response affects your relationship toward your Creator and the spirit realm.*

# CHAPTER 14

# *How The Wounded Spirit Works*
## *A Review*

*E*motional wounding and pain channels itself through an *internal emotional reactionary process* that ultimately displays itself outwardly through three distinct, external behaviors or "fruits":

*defiling the flesh* (anger, anxiety, fear, depression, abuse, etc.),
*rejecting authority* (inability to trust others), and
*reviling angelic majesties* (disregard, disrespect and disdain toward your Creator).

Each of these three behaviors directly affects and relates to your relationship with:

*yourself,*
*others around you,* and
*your Creator and the spirit realm.*

Once in a pattern of repetition, these outward behaviors become habits: *mental* habits, *emotional* habits, *physical* habits and *verbal* habits. These negative habits override your heart-nature, character and behavior, your *real*-self. They subsequently produce the outward effects of an ugly personality: bad, evil, selfish or inferior behavior. After years of living with this uncontrollable, ugly monster, you become convinced that it is a reflection of the *real* you. However, it is not. It is a reflection of the *wounded* you. Can you see this? Can you see how you have become what you are because of your *reactions* to your own pain, wounding and fear?

This emotionally transforming, metamorphic process is multi-leveled, multi-tiered. Once the initial wounding takes root as a wounded spirit, your *emotional*-self triggers a cycled progression of emotional and attitudinal reactions that eventually become part of your habit behavior. Since we are not dealing with only one or two emotional reactions (we are dealing with several in a cycled progression), our attempts to find genuine and permanent healing and change often end in futility. We usually   address one or two of the emotions, but until we address and deal with the "root," all efforts will continue to come up short of our desired goal.

So now can you see why we are often so powerless to affect genuine, permanent *emotional* change within our *emotional*-self through many of the traditional tools and means available today? Once the negative wounding has taken root and begun its cycle, we are powerless to stop this emotional progression *at any point beyond* the emotional "root." This is why so many other tools and techniques fall short of genuine and permanent change, healing, freedom and peace.

At this point, you may not be able to identify with every stage or reaction that we have discussed in the wounded "tree," or wounded *emotional*-self. This is normal. Over the years many of us *adapt* to the wounding and much of what it spawns within us. Consequently, we often are not even aware that our behavior is being controlled, influenced or directed by the negative, emotional wounds and fears of the past. However, you can know that these negative emotions are in existence because their "fruit," their outward behavior, is present in your life and life style.

Remember:

**1**. Change comes only by addressing the "*root*."

**2**. The "root" is an *emotional* issue. It is not psychological (mental), physical nor spiritual. Yet, because of the power of emotions, the problem will manifest itself, or root its tentacles (remember the plantar wart), through the three realms or "branches", of relationships within our lives.

However, permanent changes can not come by addressing an emotionally based process with a tool or technique that finds its origin in one of the other three realms of our lives—mental, physical, or spiritual. This would be like trying to repair our house's electrical problems with expertise, training, tools and principles of plumbing (remember Chapter Five). Many of us do this all the time, don't we?

Illus. 14–1: **A House With Four Parts**

### Apples and Oranges

For illustration, let's say that the "real" you, the you created in love, freedom and peace (the you before wounding entered your life), by design, produces *apples* as your emotional fruit. However, because of the wounding and pain, your emotional "tree" is producing *oranges*. Now society, your family, and your religious background all may tell you that you should be producing *apples*. So you know something is wrong. You know you stand out. So, what do you do?

Usually, when you feel no one is looking, you cut off all of the oranges and tape on dozens of apples. Relief!

However, it doesn't last long. Why? Because, there is no life in the apples. They are not *connected* to the "root," the source of life for the fruit. So, the apples soon wither and fall off. With this, your reaction is:

*"Well, that is OK. Just as long as the oranges don't return. At least my defectiveness will not be so obvious to others around me."*

But, guess what happens? Somewhere down the road of your life, sometime in the not so distant future,

Illus. 14–2: **Apples and Oranges**

someone comes along or something happens in your life which brushes against your wounding. When your wounding is touched off it produces negative feelings, fears and emotions (the progressive process we all go through emotionally through the tree—Chapters Seven through Thirteen) and before you know it, your wounded *emotional*-self is producing the negative or wounded emotional fruit (oranges) faster than you can imagine. You can't stop it. It is all on its own. It is a self-producing monster. This emotional process occurs often throughout your life. Over the years it leaves you feeling hopeless and defeated. You feel you have no say-so or control over what your feelings do, or how they will react at any given moment.

This is the reality of the *wounded* you.

This is how wounding works.

This is how your feelings, behavior and life transform and change for the worse.

But life doesn't have to be lived like this. You and I *do* have a choice. We do not have to relinquish ourselves over to an emotional hell.

At this point you may be asking, "What else is there?" "What would emotional love, healing, freedom and peace *feel* like?" We will discover the answers to these questions in Part III. However, before we look at the *real*-self in Part III, lets look at the lives of three individuals and see just how the wounded-self affects and alters a person*'s life*. Observing each of their emotional reactions to their particular circumstances will give us further insight into ourselves. We will also gain greater insight into how wounding works within those around us.

### How Wounding Works:  Three Examples

As we discussed in Chapter Seven the emotions we feel and experience are universal.  Our *reactions* to circumstances and events in our lives are unique to each of us.  However, the emotions we experience in reaction to our circumstances and events are *not* unique—they are universal.

In other words, a loved one's death may ultimately produce outward emotional "fruit" of anger within one person.  Yet, the experience of the death of a loved one may trigger wounded emotions of fear in another.  The feelings of anger and the feelings of fear are universal.  But the events that trigger each feeling or fear, and how we *react* to those external triggers, *are* unique to each of us.

To better clarify how the wounding process channels itself through the *emotional*-self, lets look at three separate circumstances encountered by three different individuals.  The people we are observing are Angela, Trevor and Sharon.  Each of these people experienced an event in their lives that was emotionally painful.  Let's look at them individually and watch how external events affected their *emotional*-self and triggered a wounded spirit within each of them.

**Angela**
**How a loved one's death produces a life style of anger**

As early as she can remember, Angela was always "daddy's little girl." She brought an extra spark into her father's life and everyone knew it. His affection for Angela was so obvious. His countenance changed whenever Angela entered his presence. Angela knew she was special in her father's eyes. She truly treasured the relationship she had with her father.

When she was nine, Angela came home from school one day to learn that her father was suddenly gone. With no advanced warning, he had died of a heart attack. This loss was more than Angela could handle, emotionally. The event of her father's death triggered a wounded spirit within Angela's *emotional*-self.

The death of the father

➡ triggers

➡ a *Wounded Spirit*

With this, Angela finds herself asking:
*"Why is this happening to me?*
*"Why did this happen to my father?"*

For Angela, the pain and loss are so intense. She seems to live from day-to-day in emotional numbness. As she grows older, Angela's reactions to the wounded spirit are feelings of *Bitterness.*

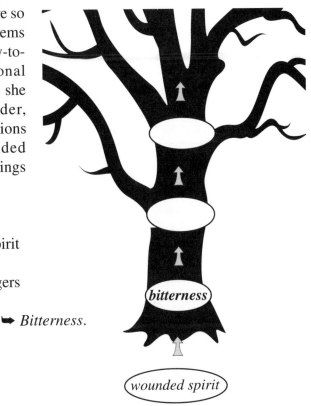

A Wounded Spirit

➡ triggers

➡ *Bitterness.*

In this emotional stage, Angela finds herself asking:
*"Why did God let this happen?*
*"Why is God causing me so much pain?*
*"If God loves us so much, why did he take my father away?"*
As a result of this, a bitterness takes root within Angela's *emotional*-self, her heart. This bitterness is directed toward her Creator. But, her emotional wounding doesn't end here. As a matter of fact, because of how she is *reacting* to the external trigger (her father's death), an emotional *chain-reaction* is occurring within Angela's *emotional*-self. New feelings and emotions emerge in *reaction* to emotions already being experienced.

Now with bitterness being firmly entrenched within her heart, Angela's *emotional*-self reacts to the feelings of bitterness with feelings of *Self-Centeredness.*

Bitterness

→ triggers

→ *Self-Centeredness.*

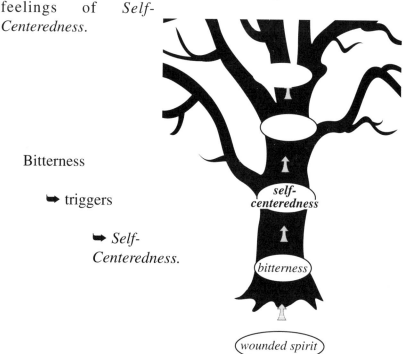

Because of the internal emotional pain, and the feelings of loss, Angela's *emotional*-self reacts to the feelings of bitterness with self-centeredness and self-preservation.  At this stage Angela finds herself thinking things like:

*"No one (including God) cares about me.*
*"If they did, I would not have to experience all of this pain.*
*"Since there is no one else who will care for me, I am going to look out for myself."*

Angela develops a self-focused life style.  This is not displayed in a cocky arrogance, though.  Angela's self-focused life style is one of turning inward, out of fear and a desire to preserve and protect herself, *emotionally*.  She has an internal drive to protect herself from further unannounced losses and hurts.  She shuts down her ability to be free, open and at peace.

Angela's heart then *reacts* to the feelings that accompany her self-centeredness with feelings of *Rebellion*.

Self-centeredness

➡ triggers

➡ *Rebellion*.

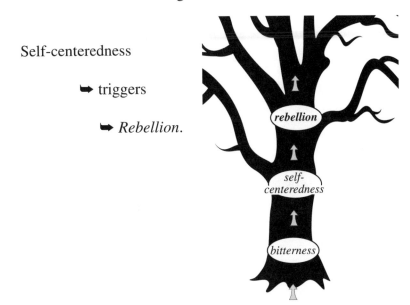

Angela's rebellion is directed to-ward her Creator. However, it is not an outward, demonstrative rebellion. Angela's rebellion is very hidden and subtle. No one but Angela is aware of its existence. It is a *masked resistance* toward her Creator. With it, Angela has thoughts like:

> *"Why should I care about God?*
> *"Look at what He has done to me and my family (the death of her father)."*

Angela's rebellion, or masked resistance, is also ultimately directed toward authority figures in her life as she experiences puberty and matures into her adulthood. Because of the male dominated society within which Angela lives, her heart grows to resist and resent male authorities in her life, much more so than just authorities in general. These feelings and attitudes all occur within the "rebellion" stage of Angela's *emotional*-self.

From here, the rebellion may manifest itself through one, two or all three of the next stages, or "branches," within Angela's *emotional*-self. Each of these three "branches" relates to Angela's feelings and attitudes toward:

> herself,
> her relationship with others and
> her Creator.

Angela's rebellion manifests itself through all three branches. Let's look at the "branch" that is directed toward herself.

At this stage in her emotional life, Angela develops an angry, critical and even mean attitude and disposition toward her Creator, toward herself and toward others. She develops a very negative outlook on life. Angela *blames* her Creator for her pain, for the meanness and cruelty of men and other women, and for the negative circumstances that always seem to plague her life.

Angela also has a difficult time maintaining good, positive, healthy relationships because of her anger. Her friends label her as being *short-fused*.

In addition to this, because of the unresolved feelings and questions associated with her father's untimely death and disappearance from her life, Angela feels intense anger and resentment toward her Creator.

At this point Angela's *emotional*-self produces an outward behavioral "fruit" of *Anger*.

For the sake of brevity, we will not explain how the anger "branches" through Angela's relationships with others or with her Creator. But the picture of this emotional process is clear, isn't it?

Now, do you see how this entire emotional process, or chain-reaction, happens? Can you see how an external event (the death of a loved one in this example), can set up an emotional chain-reaction within the *emotional*-self that ultimately manifests itself through outward behaviors of *anger*? Can you see how the "root" of the death of a loved one (which caused a wounded spirit) develops into the "fruit" of anger which, when left unchecked, will inevitably "defile the flesh"—destroy some part of the human entity, either mentally, emotionally, physically or spiritually?

To make matters worse, when the anger is repeated often enough, it eventually becomes *habit*. Consequently, feelings of anger, rage and displays of anger become a part of Angela's *behavioral habit life style*. At this point she is powerless to cut it off, eliminate it or change it by any means known to man, except by first dealing with the "root" and replacing the habit with another, more healthy habit. Can you see why most of our attempts at healing and behavioral change fall short?

So, in this example with Angela, the death of a loved one *triggered* a wounded spirit that manifested itself through outward "fruits" or behaviors of anger. This anger, once repeated often enough, became a part of Angela's habit life style. Can you imagine what it is like having to live with, be married to, or be parented by Angela? From Angela's perspective, can you imagine what it is like having to live with this internal emotional torment day after day with no hope or promise of relief or change for the better?

This is Angela's dilemma. It also is the dilemma of millions of others.

### Trevor
#### How a parents' divorce produces a life style of depression
It could be said that Trevor has had two lives. One came before his parents' divorce; the other came after his parents' divorce. Before the divorce, Trevor was happy, energetic and outgoing. He loved life and enjoyed it to the fullest. Trevor's second life was radically different from his first life. His second life developed *after* his parents divorced. With this event, an emotional transformation was set in motion that forever changed Trevor and the way he saw himself, others around him, his

Creator and life in general. In his second life, Trevor became withdrawn, quiet and inactive.

Trevor's second life began when he was only twelve. He and his brothers knew their parents were having problems. But they never realized it would lead to the elimination of their family as a unit. The event of his parents' divorce triggered a wounded spirit within Trevor's *emotional*-self.

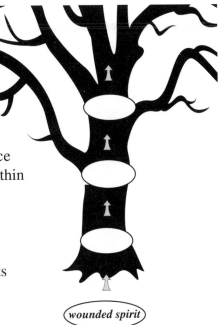

The divorce of the parents

➡ triggers

*wounded spirit*

➡ a *Wounded Spirit*

With this, Trevor finds himself asking:
*"Why is this happening to me?*
*"Why are my parents doing this?*
*"Why can't they just make up?*
*"Why can't they just get along?*
*"Surely, things couldn't be this bad, could they?"*
*"What have I done to cause this?*
*"If only I had done what they told me to do, maybe they would not have argued and fought so much."*

Trevor can find no legitimate answers that satisfy his questions and the felt void that accompanies his heart. With this, Trevor begins questioning his own role in the divorce. Consequently, he starts doubting the goodness and ability of his own personhood.

For Trevor the pain and loss are so intense.  He seems to live from day-to-day in emotional numbness.  He spends his days daydreaming while he is in school.  Consequently, his grades suffer.  As he grows older, Trevor's reactions to the wounded spirit are feelings of *Bitterness*.

A Wounded Spirit

➡ triggers

➡ *Bitterness*.

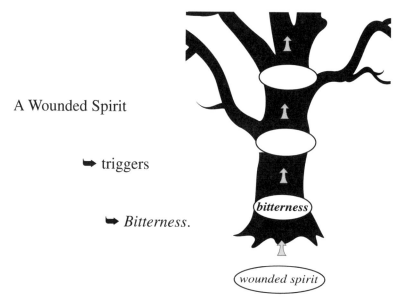

In this emotional stage, Trevor finds himself asking:

*"Why  do they (his parents) have to cause so much pain and destruction for everyone?*

*"Can't they see what they are doing to us kids?*

*"Why do they have to ruin my life and my brothers' lives?*

*"Why do they have to have so much control over my life?"*

As a result of this, a bitterness takes root within Trevor's *emotional*-self, his heart.  This bitterness is directed toward his parents.  He is bitter because of a lack of felt control over his own circumstances.  But, his emotional wounding doesn't end here.  As a matter of fact, because of how he is *reacting* to the external trigger (his parents' divorce), an emotional *chain-reaction* is occurring within Trevor's *emotional*-self.  New feelings and emotions emerge in *reaction* to emotions already being experienced.

Now with bitterness being firmly entrenched within his heart, Trevor's *emotional*-self reacts to the feelings of bitterness with feelings of *Self-Denial*.

Bitterness

➡ triggers

➡ *Self-Denial*.

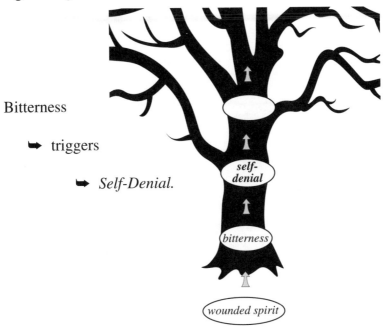

Because of the internal emotional pain, and feelings and fears of rejection and abandonment, Trevor's *emotional*-self reacts to the feelings of bitterness with self-denial and self-preservation. At this stage, Trevor finds himself thinking things like:

*"My parents must be right in their words and actions. Surely I am wrong. Surely I am to blame for all of this. My mother always says my father uses me to get at her. So I must be to blame. Why else would they do these things (the divorce)?"*

With this, Trevor begins denying and discounting his own thoughts, feelings and opinions. He concludes he is at fault, and therefore, others' opinions and assessments are more accurate than his could ever be. Ultimately, a fear-based life style develops. Trevor doubts, and consequently, fears that his own instincts are inadequate and inferior to the opinions and instincts of others.

Trevor's heart then reacts to the feelings that accompany his self-denial with feelings of *Compliance*.

Self-denial

➡ triggers

➡ *Compliance.*

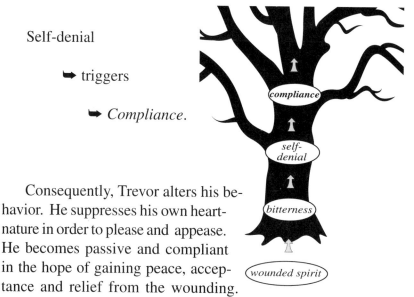

Consequently, Trevor alters his behavior. He suppresses his own heart-nature in order to please and appease. He becomes passive and compliant in the hope of gaining peace, acceptance and relief from the wounding. Trevor's compliance affects every facet of his life. It is very obvious. With it he thinks:

"*I must have been the cause of their problem.*

"*If they had not had to yell at me so much for my messy room and poor grades (he made B's), I'm sure this would not have happened.*

"*Why does my mother keep yelling at me and cursing me?*

"*I've got to do whatever it takes to make both of them happy and calm. I can't afford to upset either of them ever again.*

"*I can't afford to have my mother leave me too.*"

From here, the compliance may manifest itself through one, two or all three of the next stages, or "branches" within Trevor's *emotional*-self. Each of these three "branches" relate to Trevor's feelings and attitudes toward:

himself,

his relationship with others and

his Creator.

Initially Trevor's compliance manifests itself through the "branch" that is directed toward himself—*a lack of responsibility.*

At this stage in his emotional life, Trevor develops a lack of emotional responsibility. He looks to others for his sense of:

who he is,
how he feels,
and
for the negative circumstances surrounding his life.

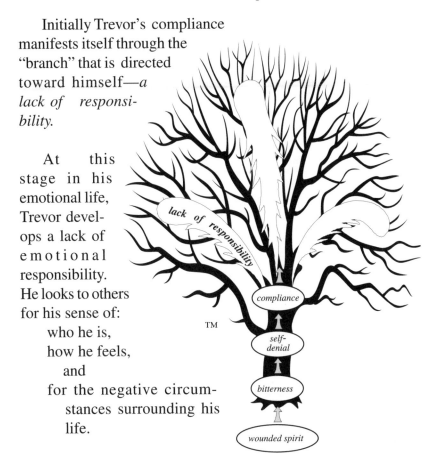

He feels that he did not bring the pain and problems into his life; others did. So, in Trevor's mind, others are in control of his life and feelings, he is not. Consequently, Trevor never feels he has any kind of a say-so in his own life. He believes that others, including his Creator, have much more of a determination over his feelings, attitudes and circumstances than he does. As a result, Trevor lives with the emotional bedfellows of hopelessness, defeat, discouragement and despair. At this point, Trevor enters the threshold of *depression* and *depressive behavior*. In short, Trevor's wounded spirit (triggered by his parents' divorce during his childhood) manifests itself through *depression*.

Trevor's depression affects his feelings and attitude toward himself. On the outer surface, Trevor appears to be undisciplined. He doesn't groom himself well. His sleep schedule is very erratic. He can never seem to hold a job for any measure of time. He never seems to be happy or satisfied. He does not like or feel good about himself or his life. To Trevor, his future feels hopeless.

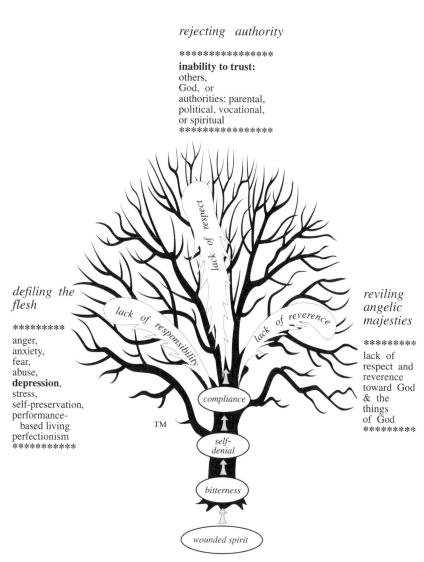

*rejecting   authority*

\*\*\*\*\*\*\*\*\*\*\*\*\*\*\*\*
**inability to trust:**
others,
God,  or
authorities: parental,
political, vocational,
or spiritual
\*\*\*\*\*\*\*\*\*\*\*\*\*\*\*\*

*lack of respect*

*defiling the flesh*

\*\*\*\*\*\*\*\*\*
anger,
anxiety,
fear,
abuse,
**depression**,
stress,
self-preservation,
performance-
  based living
perfectionism
\*\*\*\*\*\*\*\*\*\*

*lack of responsibility*

*lack of reverence*

*reviling angelic majesties*

\*\*\*\*\*\*\*\*\*
lack of
respect and
reverence
toward God
& the
things
of God
\*\*\*\*\*\*\*\*\*

*compliance*

TM

*self-denial*

*bitterness*

*wounded spirit*

Trevor's depression affects his relationship and interaction with other people. He is not very sociable. He is labeled a loner by many. Because of his emotional pain and wounding, Trevor carries a deep-seeded mistrust toward others. So his ability to have close, meaningful relationships is hindered.

Trevor's depression also affects his ability to feel a "connection" and closeness with his Creator. At the mere thought of God, Trevor's *emotional*-self reacts with feelings and thoughts of:

*"If God loves me so much, then why is He allowing so much pain in my life?"*

Out of self-protection and self-preservation, this question and many other unanswered questions cause Trevor to distance himself from his Creator. Eventually, Trevor's depression affects the relationships in all three "branches" of his life.

Do you see how this entire emotional process, or chain-reaction happens? Can you see how an external event (the divorce of one's parents in this example) can set up an emotional chain-reaction within the *emotional*-self that ultimately manifests itself through outward behaviors of *depression*? Can you see how the "root" of a divorce (which caused a wounded spirit) develops into the "fruit" of depression which, when left unchecked, will inevitably "defile the flesh"—destroy some part of the human entity, either mentally, emotionally, physically or spiritually?

To make matters worse, when this depression and depressive behavior are repeated often enough, they eventually become *habits*. Consequently, hopelessness, depression and depressive behavior become a part of Trevor's *behavioral habit life style*. At this point he is powerless to cut it off, eliminate it or change it by any means known to man, except by first dealing with the "root" and replacing the habit with another, more healthy habit. Can you see why most of our attempts at healing and behavioral change fall short?

So, in this example with Trevor, the divorce of his parents *triggered* a wounded spirit that manifested itself through outward "fruits" or behaviors of depression. This depression, once repeated often enough, became a part of Trevor's habit life style. Can you imagine what it is like having to live with, be married to, or be parented by Trevor? From Trevor's perspective, can you imagine what it is like having to live with this internal emotional torment day after day with no hope or promise of relief or change for the better?

This is Trevor's dilemma. It is also the dilemma of millions of others.

### Sharon
### How sexual abuse produces a life style of fear

Sharon doesn't remember anything in her early childhood except fear. From her earliest memories, she has lived with fear:

fear of men,
fear of inferiority,
fear of failure,
fear of inadequency,
fear of rejection, and
fear of impending doom.

Fear plagues Sharon's life. It controls every aspect of her being: mentally, emotionally, physically and spiritually.

The fear began at an extremely early age for Sharon. From the ages of three through six, Sharon experienced inappropriate physical and sexual contact by an older male. She was told to never tell anyone or else something terrible would happen to her parents.

The whole event (in this case it was a series of occurrences) caused Sharon to develop feelings of feeling dirty, unclean, impure and bad. Because of the physical abuse and violations, Sharon grew up convinced that she was bad. *Emotionally*, the physical and sexual abuse was more than Sharon could handle.

The event of the sexual abuse triggered a wounded spirit within Sharon's *emotional*-self.

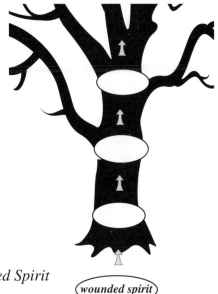

The sexual abuse

    ➡ triggers

        ➡ a *Wounded Spirit*

Sharon finds herself asking:
*"Why is this happening to me?"*
*"Why is he (the older male) doing these things to me?"*

Sharon's emotional pain is more intense than the physical pain and violation. She lives day-to-day in emotional numbness. As she grows older, Sharon's reactions to the wounded spirit are feelings of *Bitterness*.

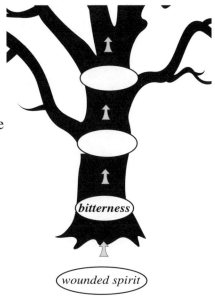

A Wounded Spirit

    ➡ triggers

        ➡ *Bitterness.*

In this emotional stage, Sharon finds herself asking:

*"Why did God let this happen?*

*"Why is God causing me so much pain?*

*"When will this happen again?*

*"If I am not careful, God will let something else, equally as bad, happen to me."*

As a result of this, a bitterness takes root within Sharon's *emotional*-self, her heart. This bitterness is directed toward men and toward her Creator. But, her emotional wounding doesn't end here. As a matter of fact, because of how she is *reacting* to the external trigger (the physical abuses and violations), an emotional *chain-reaction* is occurring within Sharon's *emotional*-self. New feelings and emotions emerge in *reaction* to emotions already being experienced. Each subsequent feeling and reaction is more detrimental and unhealthy than the previous feeling.

Now with bitterness being firmly entrenched within her heart, Sharon's *emotional*-self reacts to the feelings of bitterness with feelings of *Self-Centeredness*.

Bitterness

➡ triggers

➡ *Self-Centeredness.*

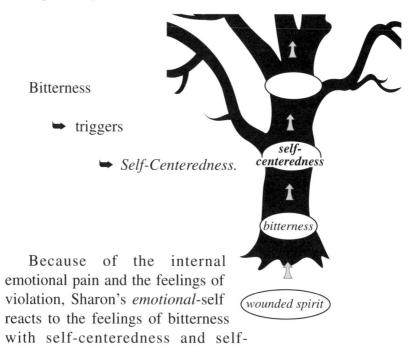

Because of the internal emotional pain and the feelings of violation, Sharon's *emotional*-self reacts to the feelings of bitterness with self-centeredness and self-preservation. At this stage Sharon finds herself thinking things such as:

*"No one (including God) cares about me.*

*"If they did, I would not have to experience all of this pain.*

*"Since there is no one else who will care for me, I am going to look out for myself."*

She develops a self-focused life style. Why? Because she now carries a feeling and attitude of *fear* with her at all times. Sharon's fear is the fear of impending doom and disaster.

The self-centeredness is not displayed in a cocky arrogance, though. Sharon's self-focused life style is one of turning inward, out of fear and a desire to preserve and protect herself, *emotionally*, as well as physically. She has an internal drive to protect herself from further unannounced violations and pains. Consequently, she shuts down her ability to be free, open and at peace.

Sharon's heart then reacts to the feelings that accompany her self-centeredness with feelings of *Rebellion*.

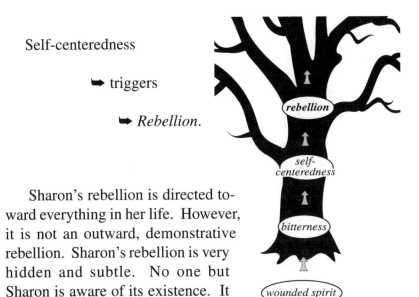

Self-centeredness

➡ triggers

➡ *Rebellion.*

Sharon's rebellion is directed toward everything in her life. However, it is not an outward, demonstrative rebellion. Sharon's rebellion is very hidden and subtle. No one but Sharon is aware of its existence. It is a *masked resistance* toward everything and everyone in her life. She has a very difficult time trusting other people, for fear of being violated again. These feelings and attitudes all occur within the "rebellion" stage of Sharon's *emotional*-self.

From here, the rebellion may manifest itself through one, two, or all three of the next stages, or "branches" within Sharon's *emotional*-self. Each of these three "branches" relate to Sharon's feelings and attitudes toward:

> herself,
>
> her relationships with others and
>
> her Creator.

Sharon's rebellion manifests itself through the branch that is directed toward herself.

At this stage in her emotional life, Sharon develops a fear-based life style. She does everything with fear as the primary motivator. She constantly reacts to her feelings of fear. She will go a hundred miles out of her way just to avoid the feelings of fear. Sharon lives with a constant *fear of failure* and inadequacy. This fear affects every thought, every action and every word that comes from Sharon's being. Interestingly, during her younger years, Sharon was not even aware that fear was controlling and directing her outward behavior. It was not a conscious reality. It was not until her middle-aged years that Sharon realized how so much of her life and life style were affected and influenced by fear and fear-based decision-making.

Sharon has a difficult time maintaining good, positive, healthy relationships because of her fear. Her friends label her as being too cautious and reserved. She has a difficult time being able to trust others. She fears she will somehow be violated again. She

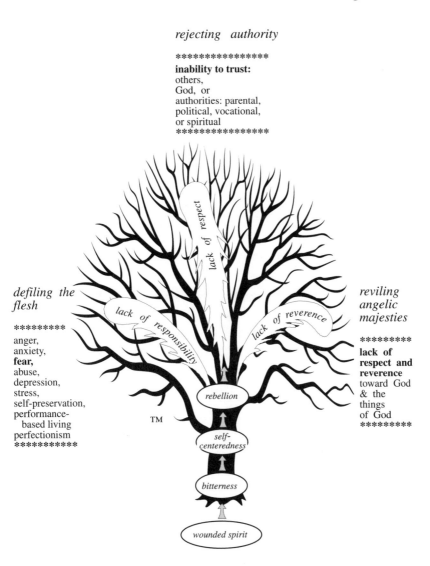

*rejecting   authority*

\*\*\*\*\*\*\*\*\*\*\*\*\*\*\*\*
**inability to trust:**
others,
God, or
authorities: parental,
political, vocational,
or spiritual
\*\*\*\*\*\*\*\*\*\*\*\*\*\*\*\*

lack of respect

*defiling the flesh*

\*\*\*\*\*\*\*\*\*
anger,
anxiety,
**fear,**
abuse,
depression,
stress,
self-preservation,
performance-
  based living
perfectionism
\*\*\*\*\*\*\*\*\*\*

lack of responsibility

lack of reverence

*reviling angelic majesties*

\*\*\*\*\*\*\*\*\*
**lack of respect and reverence**
toward God
& the
things
of God
\*\*\*\*\*\*\*\*\*

rebellion

TM

self-centeredness

bitterness

wounded spirit

also lives with the constant feeling that she will be rejected; especially if she does not do or perform to others' expectations. Sharon lives with a *fear of people* and a *fear of rejection*.

Sharon also lives with intense feelings of fear toward her Creator. She sees him as a mean, angry, wrathful God. She is convinced that He is out to get her. She is afraid of making one false move. She is certain that only doom and disaster are coming her way in the future. She has a *fear of impending doom.*

So, do you see how this entire emotional process, or chain-reaction happens? Can you see how an external event (physical and sexual abuse in this example) can set up an emotional *chain-reaction* within the *emotional*-self that ultimately manifests itself through outward behaviors of *fear*? To make matters worse, when this fear is repeated often enough, it eventually becomes *habit*. Consequently, fear and fear-based living become a part of Sharon's *behavioral habit life style*. Can you see how the "root" of abuse (which caused a wounded spirit) develops into the "fruit" of fear which, when left unchecked, will inevitably "defile the flesh"—destroy some part of the human entity, either mentally, emotionally, physically or spiritually?

At this point Sharon is powerless to cut it off, eliminate it or change it by any means known to man, except by first dealing with the root and replacing the habit with another, more healthy habit. Can you see why most of our attempts at healing and behavioral change fall short?

So, in this example with Sharon, physical and sexual abuse triggered a wounded spirit. The wounded spirit then manifests itself through outward "fruits" or behaviors of fear. This fear, once repeated often enough, becomes a part of Sharon's habit life style. Can you imagine what it is like having to live with, be married to or be parented by Sharon? From Sharon's perspective, can you imagine what it is like having to live with this internal emotional torment day after day with no hope or promise of relief or change for the better?

This is Sharon's dilemma. It also is the dilemma of millions of others.

However, life does not have to be this way. You and I can have a determination in our feelings and how we feel. Once we learn the mysteries (how our heart or *emotional*-self works), and have the necessary tools (emotionally based tools and principles), we can determine and dictate much of what our *emotional*-self will experience throughout our life and it's encounters. And we will not have to become a hermit, isolating or protecting ourselves from the real world.

There is another life. I refer to it as "The Other Side of Life." It is life as life was *intended* to be. It is life being lived as the *real* you. It is life free from the power *and* control of the *wounded* you. We explore the realities of "The Other Side of Life" in Part III of *A Journey to the Other Side of Life*.

 *Review*

# Part II

Before moving on to "Part III: The Other Side of Life," let's review what we have discussed in "Part II: The Wounded-Self":

### Chapter Seven:

## *An Invasion of the Heart*
### *The Emotional-Self is Like a Tree*

1. Emotional feelings are universal.
2. Most of our inner conflicts and problems stem from our *emotional*-self and, therefore, are *emotional in nature*, not physical, spiritual or psychological.
3. Like a tree, the *emotional*-self is a multi-level, multi-sectioned entity within each of us.
4. An emotional metamorphosis begins when wounding enters our lives.

### Chapter Eight:

## *Where It All Began: The Root*
### *The Wounded Spirit*

1. An emotional metamorphosis begins within us when wounding enters our lives.
2. This wounding, when at the "root" or core of our *emotional*-self, produces a "wounded spirit."
3. The "wounded spirit," like the roots of a tree, produces a cycled progression of negative and detrimental feelings and attitudes. These feelings and attitudes are *reactions* to the pain and wounding. These emotional reactions trigger yet *additional* emotions and attitudes, which ultimately consummate as external "fruit," or behavior. All of these feelings and attitudes ultimately become behavioral *habits*.

### Chapter Nine:

## *What Went Wrong: The Trunk*
### *Bitterness, Self-Centeredness and Rebellion—*
### *Self-denial and Compliance*

1. A *wounded spirit* produces feelings and attitudes of *bitterness*.
2. *Bitterness* produces feelings and attitudes of *self-centeredness* or (*self-denial*).
3. *Self-centeredness* produces feelings and attitudes of *rebellion* or (*compliance*).

4. This process is *emotional*, not physical, mental, or spiritual, in nature. However, it almost always will affect the mental, physical, and spiritual areas of our lives. It controls our feelings and attitudes. When often repeated, these feelings and attitudes become behavioral *habits*.

**Chapter Ten:**
## The Mystery Revealed: Three Fruits
### Our Wounded Outward Behavior

1. Our emotional wounding, once entering the stage of rebellion, will channel itself through three distinct "branches."
2. The three branches are related to and connected with the three basic realms of relationship in our lives.
3. Once through the branches, our wounding and pain will ultimately conclude its journey by thrusting itself out of our being through three distinct aspects of outward behavior, or "fruits."
4. The three distinct, outward "fruits" are:
   defiling the flesh,
   rejecting authority, and
   reviling angelic majesties.

**Chapter Eleven:**
## A Lack of Responsibility:
## The First Branch
### The Wounded-Self

1. Emotional wounding and pain, once progressed to the stage of rebellion, will manifest itself through three "branches," all of which spawn outward behaviors.
2. The first "branch" is "A Lack of Responsibility," personally.
3. This emotionally irresponsible approach to life will often lead to fear, anger or depression.
4. This "branch" of emotional irresponsibility always produces outward behaviors or "fruits" that, when left to themselves, uncontrolled, will "defile the flesh"; that is they will destroy the *real* you either mentally, physically, emotionally or spiritually.
5. This "fruit" is directed toward your self.

**Chapter Twelve:**
## A Lack of Respect:
## The Second Branch
### The Wounded-Self

1. The second "branch" is "A Lack of respect," toward others.

2. This "lack of respect" approach to life exists because of an inability to *trust* others.

3. This inability to trust others produces a "fruit" of "rejection of authority."

4. When left unbridled and uncontrolled, this emotional "fruit" inevitably ruins and destroys your friendships and relationships.

5. This "fruit" affects your relationship with others around you.

**Chapter Thirteen:**

## *A Lack of Reverence:*
### *The Third Branch*
#### *The Wounded-Self*

1. The third "branch" is "A Lack of Reverence" *toward your Creator.*

2. This "lack of reverence" approach to life exists because of a lack of respect toward your Creator and His ways.

3. This inability to respect and revere your Creator produces a fruit of "reviling (mocking) angelic majesties (spirit realm)."

4. When left unbridled and uncontrolled, this emotional "fruit" inevitably ruins and destroys your relationship and felt "*connection*" with your Creator.

5. This third "fruit" or emotional response affects your relationship toward your Creator and the spirit realm.

# Part III

## *The Other Side of Life*

### YOUR REAL-SELF
#### The Whole & Healed You

*"Above all else, guard your heart,*
*for it influences everything else in your life."*

*"A tree is identified by its fruit.*
*A tree from a select variety produces good fruit;*
*poor varieties don't."*

*"Happy are those whose hearts are pure,*
*for they shall see God."*
**The Bible**

# CHAPTER 15

## *Holiness: The Root*
### The Other Side of Life

*"Long ago, even before He made the world, God chose us to be His very own, through what Christ would do for us; He decided then to make us holy in His eyes."*
**The Bible**

 This is the other side of life. This is how your life is supposed to be. This is the way things should have been before fear and wounding and negative feelings and emotions took over and changed what you do, say, think and feel. This is the way you were before wounding set in and altered your behavior: your mental, emotional, physical and verbal behavior.

This is life free of fear and wounding. This is a life of love, healing, freedom and peace. This is the way life is meant to be. This is an *emotional* life that consistently produces feelings and emotions of peace, patience, self-control, love, gentleness, kindness, faithfulness, joy and goodness within you. This is a way of life that allows you to enjoy healthy, fulfilling relationships. In this way of life, you have the ability to find and experience your purpose and personal identity. This life gives your heart the freedom to feel a *connection* with the One who created you. It truly is the other side of life.

### "Fruit" is Produced, Not Acquired

So, how does a life that is free from fear, anger, depression and wounding produce emotions of peace, love, joy, self-control, patience, kindness, gentleness and goodness? These are qualities that we all pursue throughout our entire lives. So how does it happen? How can these felt emotional experiences be acquired?

First of all, you can not *acquire* them. You can not buy or wear them like a suit of clothes. Many have tried this approach for centuries. It never has worked. It doesn't work today. The essence behind most counseling, therapy, positive thinking, self-help and self-improvement revolves around this faulty approach. That is why so much of what we have tried before now has not permanently lasted within our lives.

The reason that the approaches mentioned above have not produced permanent, genuine, long-lasting and positive change and healing is because the focus has been skewed. By nature we try to produce change by altering the outward fruit. It doesn't work. It may seem to work. However, the effect is only temporary. Before long, the old thoughts, feelings, words and actions resurface. You can not make an orange tree become an apple tree simply by lopping off the oranges and pasting on apples (remember this illustration from Chapter Fourteen). The futility of this exercise is obvious, isn't it? Yet, this is exactly what we try to do with regard to our *emotional*-self throughout our lives. However, it never works, permanently.

How can you or I produce these positive, healthy emotional experiences on a normal and consistent basis within our heart, mind and life? Again, we must focus on the "root" or core of the *emotional*-self to find the answer. At the root or core of the *emotional*-self, a felt sense of *holiness* must be seeded, watered, nurtured and firmly rooted (see Illus. 15–1).

# The *Real*-Self
## *The Whole & Healed Emotional-Self*

Illus. 15–1: **Holiness: The Real-Self.**

## What is Holiness?

What is holiness?  First of all let's clear up what holiness is *not*.  It is not merely some religious term.  It is not a plateau of spiritual piety to be attained or acquired.  Those of us with any type of religious background will almost always see holiness purely from a religious or spiritual focus.  When we do this we *limit* the essence of holiness.  We limit its power to change and influence our lives.  Holiness is much more than something spiritual or religious.  Holiness is a felt *emotional* experience as well.

So, experientially speaking, what is holiness?  Holiness is a felt sense of *wholeness* and *completeness*.  When you have holiness within, you *feel* whole, complete, lacking in nothing:  mentally, emotionally, physically and spiritually.

Holiness is not just purity.  However, holiness *drives* you and compels you *toward* purity.  Purity is a natural desire when holiness is resident within your *emotional*-self.  But again, holiness is not purity alone.  Holiness is a felt sense of wholeness and completeness.

So, if holiness can not be acquired, and if it can only be produced from within, what can we do within ourselves to produce the felt emotions of holiness consistently throughout our lifetime?

## Five Keys For Emotional Holiness

There are *five keys* that produce emotional holiness.  At the heart of our counseling/life-improvement process, which we call the Journey, is the engrafting of these five keys into one's life style.  The engrafting of these keys, along with other aspects of emotional healing,  life-improvement and change,  is what this Journey is mostly about.

Five Keys For Emotional Holiness:

      **1.** Emotional *control*
      **2.** A felt sense of *connection*
      **3.** Personal *attitude*
      **4.** Emotional *healing*
      **5.** Self-identification and *purpose*

When you walk through your own emotional Journey out of wounding and into love, healing, freedom and peace, you experience three distinct phases to your own emotional healing, change and transformation. As you walk through the first of these three phases, you experience the first three "keys" listed above: emotional *control*, a sense of *connection* and a changed *attitude*.

We refer to the first phase as "Relief." During this phase, over the course of several sessions, we prescribe six "foundational" assignments for the client. The counselor monitors the effect and results that each of these "foundational" assignments has on the client. We prescribe additional elements to the client when needed to bring the client to the necessary level of felt, emotional experience and change before moving through the remainder of the counseling/life-improvement process, or Journey.

The fourth key, emotional *healing*, is accomplished during the second, or middle phase of our time with the client. We refer to this phase as "Healing."

The fifth key, self-identification and *purpose*, blossoms within the client as we walk them through the final phase of our counseling/life-improvement process. We refer to this phase of the Journey as "Restoration."

Let's look more closely at the Five Keys For Emotional Holiness.

### ⚷ *1*. **Emotional Control.**

All of us have to feel a sense of *control* over our emotions and how we feel. Many do not. In order for you to feel a sense of wholeness and completeness however, you must have a sense of control over who you are and how you feel. As we have mentioned before, this comes when you take personal responsibility for who you are, how you feel and for the circumstances in your life. It is much easier *not* to take that responsibility. It is easier to blame those closest to you or to hold them responsible for who you are, how you feel or for the circumstances surrounding your life. However, when you do this, you are short-circuiting the needed, felt expression of wholeness and completeness within your life.

How? When you blame or hold others responsible for your feelings, you are giving them control of your feelings. When you give someone else the control of your feelings, you no longer have that control. You relinquish emotional control. As we learned in previous chapters, this can lead to depression.

So, for you to feel a sense of holiness—which is wholeness and completeness—emotionally, you have to live a life style of being in charge, in control and responsible for who you are, how you feel and for the circumstances in your life. Anything less than this will set you up for emotional suicide. You must be the one who is in control of who you are and how you feel.

### ⚷  *2*. **A Felt Sense of Connection.**

Everyone has to *feel connected*. This drive is within you from the womb. You look for its fulfillment from the earliest hours of your life. Most of what you do in your life today, relationally and vocationally, revolves around your pursuit of feeling *connected*. Most people feel a void or emptiness in the *emotional* area of their lives. That void is almost always tied to a felt *disconnection*, or absence of *connection*.

Even when the relationships and job environments seem to be at their best, many people still feel a loss in this area of *connection*. In an emotionally focused approach to healing and life-improvement, there is only one thing which consistently and permanently fills this void and need within the human heart.

That one thing is a sense of closeness and *connection emotionally* between us and the Creator who made us. I am not speaking from a religious perspective, though. I am speaking from a purely *emotional* perspective. So I hope you, the reader, will not react (either positively or negatively) to this idea with all of your past or present religious knowledge and experience. It is merely a statement of truth, fact and reality. Some of us are relieved to hear this. Others react violently against it. Either way, it is fact. Like it or not, we will always feel a sense of void or emptiness within our *emotional*-self until that sense of *connection* is met and fulfilled. Our counseling experiences have shown that the felt sense of *connection* can only be fulfilled genuinely through a felt closeness and connection with our Creator.

It makes perfectly logical sense. Who best would know and understand the creation but the Creator who formed the creation? The very things you pursue—closeness, understanding, acceptance and love—are all supplied to your *emotional*-self when you feel *connected* with the One who made you.

Who better would know you, understand you, accept you, love you and desire to be close to you, but the One who formed you—in His image, at that? It makes a lot of sense, doesn't it?

What does connection feel like? It feels like love. The essence of connection *is* love. From infancy, all of us naturally look to the one closest to us, usually our mother and sometimes our father, for this felt need for love. This effort works fine until the one in whom we have been looking to leaves or dies or abandons us either emotionally and/or physically—through death, divorce or personal preoccupation with their own fear, wounding and pain. Why do we look to others around us to fill our emotional needs?

First, naturally and logically it seems as though that which we can perceive through our five senses may best meet our emotional need for connection. This isn't so, of course, but intellectually it seems so. The second reason we tend to look to others around us is because we desire *love* and we desire *connection*. Connection produces love. When you feel connected, you feel love.

*However, love embodies risk and vulnerability.* Love is not passive or defensive. It requires risk and vulnerability. Such action takes strength, not weakness. People sometimes see demonstrative love as a weakness because it takes vulnerability and transparency to emit, evoke and receive love. Consequently, many conclude that such vulnerability is evidence of internal emotional weakness. It is not. Love is active. Love is assertive. Love is aggressive. It requires much more strength to be open, transparent and vulnerable, than it does to build a shell and project a false front or facade of strength. In the absence of love and connection, wounding prevails. Barricaded or barriered resistance hinders love—both love coming in and love going out.

At the Life Institute, we help our clients find and experience this need for *connection* between themselves and their Creator. For many, once the religious memories or experiences of the past and present are removed from their associations with their Creator, this sense of *connection* becomes an incredible *emotional* experience. We have learned not to take the power of *connection* lightly. It is critically important. In order for it to be engrafted within you, you have to go beyond the traditional ideas about God, religious life and spiritual communication. We do this in our counseling/life-improvement process.

When you feel *connected,* you feel loved and valued. You feel a sense of belonging. You feel hope.

So, if there is to be a consistently felt experience of holiness, or wholeness and completeness, within your heart, it will be because you are consistently feeling a sense of *connection.*

### 🔑 *3.* **Personal Attitude.**

From the womb, most of us are very hopeful and optimistic. Our hearts are filled with love and hope. This love and hope causes us to enter life with an innocent, transparent vulnerability. A transparent vulnerability is precisely what allows for fulfilling relationships. However, it is also what so easily sets us up for intense wounding and pain, especially when we are surrounded by a world of wounded people.

Because of wounding and fear, negative attitudes and pessimistic feelings displace feelings of optimism. Your emotional life is doomed when you have a pessimistic or negative outlook on life.

⇨ Life is limited, restricted and confined through pessimism.

⇨ Relationships are limited, restricted and confined by pessimism.

⇨ Dreams, goals and desires are limited, restricted and confined because of pessimism.

Pessimism works like a bitter poison on your heart, mind and life. It destroys much of what you wish to feel, experience and accomplish in your life.

Sadly though, many people feel powerless to change their outlook on life. The ability to change our attitudes is impossible for many of us, even when we know that a negative and pessimistic attitude is counterproductive to what we want to feel. A desire to see yourself, your life and others around you through a more positive perspective is not enough to produce change in your attitudinal focus. There must also be genuine and permanent healing and change, emotionally.

Attitude correlates with disposition, like the egg correlates with the chicken. You know they are related. Yet, like the chicken and the egg, which came first, the attitude or the disposition? The mere thought of it breeds confusion and frustration. Before you know it, you feel hopeless and overwhelmed. So you give up.

You can tell when people have given up on changing their attitudes. They become defensive of the pessimism or negativism. They convince themselves that being pessimistic is a good quality. They use euphemisms to lighten the blows on their own hearts. They will refer to themselves as being conservative or cautious. However, this attitude is not a true conservatism or cautiousness. This attitude perpetuates itself through thinly masked, subtle *fear*. The fear came when the wounding set in. Consequently, they feel powerless to change their attitude.

*You are powerless to change anything until you are free from the wounding and its accompanying "fruit."* It is vitally important for you to be free from emotional wounding and fear. You must be free to live and experience life with an optimistic, positive attitude and outlook. Emotional wounding hinders your ability to love, live and enjoy life to its fullest intention. Wounding causes you to adopt an attitude of guarded pessimism. The way you feel about yourself, your job, your friends, everything, is dependent on your attitude and approach to life. So, for you to have a felt sense of *holiness*—wholeness and completeness—*emotionally*, you must have a good, healthy, optimistic, positive attitude in your approach to life and living.

### ✐ 4. Emotional Healing.

As we discussed in Chapter Four, there are three sources for our emotional pain:

 ☞ *wounding,*
 ☞ *unfulfilled emotional expectations,* and
 ☞ *habits* spawned by wounding and unfulfilled
    expectations.

In order to effectively and genuinely conquer and eliminate the emotional pain, and the patterns of behavior it creates, we need to be aware of the source of that pain. In other words, to consistently feel *holiness*—wholeness and completeness—*emotionally*, it is important that we are healed of the pain and free from its source. It is just as crucial that we are set free from the habits those wounds and expectations trigger within our heart, mind and life.

### ✐ 5. Self-Identification and Purpose.

The reason many of us are so vulnerable and susceptible to wounding and violation in the first place is because we are unsure of ourselves. We don't have a clear understanding of who we are or what our *purpose* is in life. Consequently, we easily latch onto the nearest things or people around us in an attempt to find ourselves, feel good about ourselves, and feel a sense of purpose and identity. We do this either through our hobbies and jobs, or through our relationships. However, the answer for your personal identity and purpose can not be found externally. The answer lies *within* you. Who you are and your purpose for life were infused within you from the womb.

So, it is important that you know who you are and why you are alive. If you don't have these answers for your life, then it is good for you to go on your own Journey. Your Journey should be one of emotional-healing, self-discovery and purpose. When this occurs, you feel restored. Emotionally, you are restored back to the place in your life which you always knew was there, but maybe had lost touch with or maybe had never attained before. However, you always knew it was there, somewhere.

Consequently, to feel *connected*, you must also know, understand and feel a sense of identity and purpose for your life.

The Other Side of Life is a life which is first healed and free of emotional wounding, pain and fear. In addition to this, The Other Side of Life is a life of love, healing, freedom, peace and joy. These qualities are your constant emotional companions when you are feeling and experiencing feelings of *holiness*—wholeness and completeness—emotionally. These pleasurable emotional experiences are yours when you have these five keys:

   1. Emotional *control*,
   2. A felt sense of *connection*,
   3. A healthy *attitude*,
   4. Emotional *healing*, and
   5. Self-identification and *purpose*.

Once you are in this position *emotionally* (the position of felt holiness), as with the wounded-self, your *emotions* begin an emotional chain-reaction process that works through several levels within your *emotional*-self. However, this emotional chain-reaction process is good, enjoyable and pleasurable. It works *for* you, not against you. Each level, or tier, in this emotional chain-reaction process is a *reaction* to the previous level or emotion. When you reach The Other Side of Life, these emotional reactions ultimately produce life, love and liberty, *emotionally*.

As your heart feels and experiences holiness, it will react to this felt sense of holiness. The emotional reaction to holiness is the "fruit" of hope. We will discuss this "fruit," or emotional reaction, in Chapter Sixteen.

———— ⚇ ————

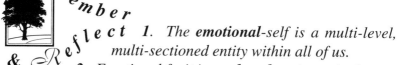

*Remember & Reflect*   1.  The **emotional**-*self is a multi-level, multi-sectioned entity within all of us.*
2. *Emotional fruit is **produced**, **not** acquired.*

3. *Within your **real**-self (the whole and healed you), the emotional "root" of your **emotional**-self is **holiness**.*

4. *Holiness is emotional **wholeness** and **completeness**.*

5. ***Five keys** stimulate and produce a felt sense of holiness:*
- *1. Emotional **control**,*
- *2. A felt sense of **connection**,*
- *3. A healthy **attitude**,*
- *4. Emotional **healing**, and*
- *5. Self-identification and **purpose**.*

# CHAPTER 16

## *Hope: The Trunk*
### *The Other Side of Life*

*"This <u>hope</u> is a strong and trustworthy <u>anchor</u> of the <u>soul.</u>"*
**The Bible**

 couple of years ago Rachel came to us for help. She had been sexually abused as a child. Over the years, she developed an emotional life style of fear and self-doubt. Rachel was constantly afraid of everything and everyone. She lived with the fear of impending doom. She expected her life to be stricken someway or somehow, at any moment.

Early in her adulthood, Rachel turned to her Creator in an attempt to conquer her emotional torment. Yet, even this failed to bring permanent relief. She was too afraid of God. She felt that even He was out to get her.

Before meeting Rachel, we had never worked with someone so extremely possessed and controlled by unfounded fear. Fear was so strong within Rachel that she virtually could not think straight or carry on a logical conversation. Her thought patterns were very disorganized. She lived in a constant state of confusion. Fear and confusion controlled every facet of her being.

When we first began working with Rachel, our thoughts were the same as they are with the majority of our clientele. We believed that once we started Rachel on a couple of our standard assignments, which we regularly prescribe to our clients, we would soon see improvement. It did not happen. Rachel came to her sessions still plagued by the same muddled confusion, terrifying fear and self-doubt.

Initially, we believed this was because she was not doing the assignments as prescribed. As we probed Rachel a little more closely, though, we found that she had done her work precisely as had been explained. This baffled us. Why wasn't she seeing the same type of improvement and change that we were accustomed to seeing? The tools and methods had already successfully proven themselves, countless times. We knew that they were not the problem. We also knew that Rachel was not the problem, either. She was not some anomaly. No one ever is, though many fear they are. She was very much like every other human being. We knew that these two factors—the tools and principles we use, and the human being we are working with— are two constants. What do we mean by this?

First, the tools and methods we work with, as we have discussed before, are based on basic laws or principles which govern the emotional realm of life. As you know, laws, whether they are physical, mental, spiritual or emotional laws, are constant and precise. They contain *no* randomness. Once we learn the boundaries and perimeters (or properties) of any given law or principle, we can count on it. For this reason, a law or principle is very *predictable* and *consistent*.

Usually, it is our *ignorance* of, or *confusion* with regard to, a given law or principle that causes us to believe there is randomness or unpredictability. However, the laws themselves are constant and consistent. Consequently, they are *predictable* and easy to follow, once we know and understand their properties.

Second, the human creation is predictable. You and I are governed by laws and principles. Physically, mentally, spiritually and emotionally we are made up of constant, consistent and predictable laws or principles. Our humanness is, therefore, not random. It is predictable, once we know, understand, and are aware of the laws and principles that govern and make up each realm of our lives. Our humanness is predictable.

With these two facts, we knew that the problem was neither the tools and methods, nor the client. What was the problem? Why hadn't our normal processes been working within Rachel?

We found that her problem was due to the emotional imbalances with which she lived. Her wounding and abuse caused her to conflict with the laws that make up the mental and emotional realm. This conflict then set off a chain-reaction (the emotional chain-reaction process discussed in Part II) that ultimately took over and controlled Rachel's mental, emotional, spiritual and physical behavior. She consequently believed, and was convinced of, things that were not true. In some instances, she believed and held to thoughts and feelings that were not even based on reality; but they *felt* real. So, she believed them.

Because of this, no matter what she did, said or experienced, the overpowering wounded feelings, fears and thoughts overrode any pleasurable, positive or hopeful thought or experience that was contrary to the negative, destructive thoughts, feelings and words. Rachel, in her current state of existence, was incapable of experiencing an ounce of hope or change for the better.

Why? Because of the fears, feelings and wounds. The problem was not because of a defect within Rachel. Nor was the problem because of a defect or flaw within the tools and principles used for healing and change. The problem was because of an invader (remember Chapter Three). This invader (the wounding) moved in and altered Rachel's behavior. This altered behavior created many emotional, physical, mental and spiritual imbalances within Rachel's life. Her imbalances were extremely severe. The severity she experienced required extreme countermeasures.

With this in mind, we custom designed our process, in the earlier stages, to fit Rachel's situation. We saw that what Rachel needed first, more than anything else, was to be able to feel *hope*.

If Rachel was able to feel hope, this hope, in turn, would cause her to question and possibly even doubt the validity and reality of the negative feelings and fears that were so deeply entrenched within her habit life style.

We gave Rachel a couple of assignments that we knew, when performed, would trigger feelings of *hope* within her. This is exactly what happened. The hope was very slight at first. However, it was enough. After a few sessions, with each session progressively building on the previous one, Rachel experienced greater increments of felt hope. Ultimately, she was able to conquer fear and get on the road toward her own healing, freedom and peace.

### Hope

*Hope* is one of the most crucial and important factors within the *emotional*-self. Without hope, we sink into *depression*. Without hope, we have no *motivation* to live another day. Without hope we struggle for a *purpose* to our lives. Hopelessness is very destructive to our physical, mental, spiritual and emotional well-being. An absence of hope causes us to experience feelings of
*isolation,*
*alienation,*
*fear (intense fear),*
*loneliness,*
*hopelessness and*
*depression.*

*Hope* is vital to your emotional, physical, relational, mental *and* spiritual well-being.

However, contrary to popular thought, being able to feel and experience hope is not a random, unpredictable variable. Because hope is an emotion, and because the emotional realm is contained within governed, predictable laws, hope can be planned out, predicted and determined. In order to do this, we simply need to know and understand what triggers or causes felt emotions of hope.

## What is Hope?

What is hope?  Hope is an internal *optimism* toward your self and your life.  It is not a cocky arrogance.  When resident within your heart, hope causes you to feel an optimistic *promise* toward yourself, your life and your future.  It causes you to feel really good about:

who you are,

why you are here on this earth, and

where you are going in life.

## An Anchor for the Soul

Hope is to your *emotional*-self what an anchor is to a ship.  An anchor provides secure, stable, steady strength for the ship as it attempts to function and exist within a vast, unpredictable, and sometimes tumultuous ocean.  In earlier days, before the arrival of inboard power, sailing ships would use their anchors to pull them through dangerous, rock-filled ravines and coastal canyons.

The captain would cast the anchor ahead of the ship and then, with sails drawn so as not to be thrust into the rocks by unexpected gusts of wind, the ship would "pull" itself to the anchor. The anchor would be cast and the ship drawn to the anchor several times.  This practice allowed the ship to move safely between and through mountainous rock cliffs, and on into a safe harbor.  Thus, the anchor would guide and lead the ship into its *harbor of safety* (see Illus. 16-1).

Illus. 16–1: **Ship/Harbor of Safety.**

Hope works in much the same way. Feelings of hope lead and guide your *emotional*-self through the dangerous, uncharted waters of life. Hope secures your protection and safety from the hidden elements of emotional danger: the rock cliffs and coastal canyons in life, relationships, jobs, activities, etc. Hope guides you safely through relationships, vocational pursuits and everyday experiences in life. Hope is your *emotional anchor.*

However, hope is not only an emotional anchor, it is also an anchor for your entire soul. From Chapter Two, we learned that you consist of several parts: a body, a spirit and a soul. The soul consists of your mind, will and emotions. So, if hope is an anchor for the soul, that means that hope is an anchor, not only for your emotions, but also for your mind. In other words, hope gives you mental, as well as emotional stability, safety and security. If you have hope, you have stability: emotionally, mentally, physically and spiritually.

### Holiness Produces Hope

In created form, apart from wounding, you and I are intended to feel and experience holiness. From the previous chapter, we learned that holiness is much more than purity and piety. Holiness is a felt emotion and sense of wholeness and completeness. It comes as we feel "connected."

When holiness is a natural part of your *emotional*-self, it will trigger, cause or produce feelings of *hope*. In other words, emotional holiness produces a natural "fruit." The "fruit" of holiness is *hope* (see Illus. 16–2).

From Chapter Fifteen, we learned of the importance of feeling a sense of *holiness*—wholeness and completeness—emotionally. These feelings of *holiness*, in turn, trigger or cause feelings of love, value, belonging, optimism and *hope*. So, if we want to feel hope, we first must be feeling a sense of *holiness*. However, as we also learned in the previous chapter, our pursuit of this emotional experience is usually short-circuited.

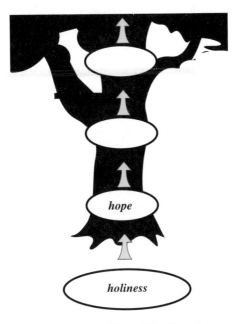

*hope*

*holiness*

Illus. 16–2: **Hope: The Trunk**

The reason for this is that we often attempt to experience holiness through a felt sense of *connection* primarily with *other humans*, who by nature are incapable of supplying us with our needed doses of stable, steady, consistent felt *connection*. The stabilizing powers resident within our Creator are what allow each of us to feel and experience the primary felt *connection* we need emotionally.

So, to feel and experience consistent feelings of *hope*, you first must be experiencing feelings of *holiness*. In order for you to feel holiness, you must first feel and experience a sense of *connection*. In order to feel and experience stable, consistent feelings of *connection*, you must feel and be *connected* with some-one in a relationship that will not fail, falter or abandon you. That relationship, emotionally (not spiritually), can only be, by nature, with the Creator who created you.

So, just as with the wounded *emotional*-self, once the healed and whole *emotional*-self (the *real*-self) is "rooted" and entrenched within your heart, it produces a cycled progression, or chain reaction *emotionally*. These feelings and emotions produce life and the zeal for living. The "root" of the healed or *real-self* is holiness. Holiness, in turn, triggers or produces feelings of hope. Hope, in turn, produces _____? Not yet! We will look into this in the next chapter.

———— ⬧ ————

*Remember & Reflect*   *1. Feeling **holiness**—wholeness and completeness—emotionally, causes you to feel feelings of **hope**.*

2. *Hope is an **internal optimism** that you feel toward yourself, your life and your future.*

3. *Hope is to your heart what an anchor is to a ship: an emotional protector from life's treacheries. Hope is an anchor for your soul (the mind, will and emotions).*

4. *Holiness produces **hope**.*

5. *This process is **emotional**, not physical, mental or spiritual, in nature. However, it almost always will affect the mental, physical and spiritual areas of our lives. It is an **emotional** process that controls your feelings and attitudes. These feelings and attitudes, repeatedly felt and experienced often enough, eventually become behavioral **habits**.*

# CHAPTER 17

## Faith: The Trunk
### The Other Side of Life

*"Having been firmly **rooted** and now being built up in Him and established in your __faith__ . . ."*

**The Bible**

 hate risks. Don't you? The mere thought of having to take a risk often knots my stomach and brings on nausea. Our cultural life style reflects our adversity to risk as a whole. We like things to be planned and predictable:

> nine to five jobs;
> easy payment plans — monthly;
> a set career path — school, college, job, retirement.

In short, we like things to be predictable and comfortable with no surprises.

However, the very thing we try to avoid—risk—many times provides us with the greatest opportunities in our lives. Taking risks often results in success, reward and growth in business, finances and relationships. In talking about humanity's adversity to risk-taking, I am reminded of a time during the younger days of my Journey through life.

Early in our marriage, my wife and I, along with our two children (we now have six children), moved to a large city in the midwestern United States. Our basis for the move was not necessarily logical or rational. We both felt that it was something we should do. We could not explain why. With such an illogical and irrational impression, we both felt as though it were a test of our faith in our unseen Creator. Were we willing to take such a risk if He asked? God often "tested" the faith of His children in the Bible—not to see if they had any faith, but to show them how much faith existed within their hearts.

Was that what was going on in our lives? We were not sure. However, we both knew we could not ignore the impression. So, ignoring our natural self-preservation instincts, we decided to leave my job and career path. We moved to a large city 1,200 miles from our nearest friends and relatives. It sounds very irrational, doesn't it?

As it turned out, it definitely was a test of our hearts. It served as a major turning point in this author's life. It set us on a course that eventually led to our move to Texas and prepared us for the career I have walked in as a counselor during the past decade. But, at the time of the move to the U.S. Midwest, we did not know that it was, or soon would be, a test.

Once we had moved, I faced the reality of financially supporting a wife and two children. Life was tough and rough to say the least, during our first few months. Our country was in the middle of an economic downturn. If it had not been for the help of newly acquired church friends, we would have suffered dearly.

As I said earlier, I knew I needed to find work to support and provide for my family. I tried a few things, but I could tell that my heart was not in any of them. After a couple of dead ends, I made a concerted effort to listen to my heart. What did my heart want to do? My heart wanted to work around airplanes. The answer was frightening, but I understood it.

I loved planes as a child. I had even taken a few flying lessons when my wife and I were first married. I loved flying. During our first year of marriage, my wife and I would park at the commercial airport and watch the aircraft land and depart.

While contemplating what I wanted to do, I began thinking about my very first church Sunday School teacher (shortly after I had experienced my spiritual awakening, at the age of seventeen, I began attending a church). Years earlier I had attended a church class. The teacher, whose name was Buddy, lived a lively life. I truly envied his life style. During the late sixties and early seventies, Buddy had been a professional golfer on the PGA tour. After several hard knocks while on the tour, including a bankruptcy and a faltering marriage, Buddy left the tour. Sometime during all of this, Buddy came into a spiritual relationship with his Creator. He worked hard to get his life on track. I often remembered how he related his own life's stories to the Bible lesson he was teaching.

Just a couple of years earlier, Buddy had been penniless. Faced with supporting a wife and children, Buddy went to the local airport and walked from hangar to hangar asking for jobs; he would do anything needed in order to provide for his family. Buddy began by washing airplanes. By the time I came into his church class, Buddy was operating a small aircraft restoration service at the airfield. He had built this business from nothing in about three years. His whole story fascinated me. A couple of years later, when I was heading off to college, Buddy *bought* an airport—*the whole thing.* In my youthful eyes, Buddy was the *epitome* of success.

Well, once my family and I were in the Midwest, 1,200 miles from all of our friends and family, I drew on my memories of Buddy and his successes. If he could do it, I could do it, too. So I did. Having no knowledge whatsoever about the aviation industry, I started an aviation company. The reason I am telling you all of this is because what happened to me between the time I decided to *start* the company and the time it finally became a success was one of the most difficult times in my life. It was a time that exercised the greatest measure of faith and *risk-taking* that had ever been required of me up to that point in my young life. That difficult time period in my life directly relates to the topic of this chapter.

Once I realized what my heart wanted to do, and having received my wife's approval and agreement to do it—we have always worked and made decisions together as a team, not as two separate individuals—I started an aviation cleaning and restoration service company. Having decided this, I began my market research. I went to the major private/corporate airfield in the city—start with the biggest, was my philosophy. I went to every aircraft dealer, retailer, and FBO (fixed base operator — these were the major lease holders at the airport, the people who lease out hangar and tie-down space to the owners of aircraft). Without exception, almost everyone I spoke with was very enthusiastic about my intentions. Several told me they would use me immediately, if only I were in business.

Also from my research, I learned that I would have only one competitor, and he was known for performing less than satisfactory work. From all of this, I drooled with excitement! Buddy's example had already demonstrated that the idea would work. The people I spoke with at the airport confirmed the need for my service. The competition was subpar in performance. I felt it was an opportunity ripe for the picking.

Boy, was I ever wrong! Getting this company off the ground turned out to be the most difficult thing I have ever had to do in my life (even to this day). For some odd reason, once I was ready to open my business, everyone who had glad-handed me when I did my research was now giving me a very cold shoulder. No one, I repeat, *no one* would have anything to do with me or my service. In retrospect, I am sure it was due to the fact that I was very new to the scene. I had no experience, and I had yet to prove my ability to anyone. I am sure people were reluctant to take the risk. Fear of failure and feelings of rejection became my constant companions.

With the cold shoulders came the haunting reality that I could not wash airplanes if I could not sell my services. I could not sell my services to anyone if I did not know the names of the aircraft owners. With the dealers, vendors and FBOs rejecting my services, who would I sell my services to? The vendors, dealers and the FBOs would not supply me with the names of their lessors of hangar or tie-down space (the owners of the airplanes who might use my services), nor did they want to use me to service their planes. What was I going to do? I remember feeling nauseated and sick for weeks as I bogged forward with this business. I had a wife and two children who needed a roof, clothes and food. I was at a point where fear was working hard against my faith and my willingness to continue taking additional emotional and physical risks.

However, I knew in my gut that this business would work if only I could acquire the names of the aircraft owners. Once aware of my services, I believed some of them would use me. Ninety-five percent of the aircraft at the airport were filthy.

One day, while pondering my dilemma with a corporate pilot at the airport, he gave me a suggestion. He said I could locate the owner of any given aircraft once I had the N-number of that particular airplane. The N-numbers are the registration numbers on the sides of every airplane. N-numbers are to airplanes what license plates are to automobiles. By law, every airplane is required to be registered, by it's N-number, with the Federal Aviation Administration (FAA). This particular pilot friend went on to tell me that the registration informtion for the N-numbers was stored on microfilm at the FAA office.

It just so happened that the local FAA office was at the same airfield from which I was attempting to start my company. So, armed with this information, I set out to record *every* N-number on *every* airplane in the airport. This was not an easy task. Many of the planes were under lock and key inside hangars. Being an "outsider," I did not have permitted access to many of the airplanes. In addition to this, I was trying to do all of this during the dead of winter. Below freezing temperatures were the normal weather diet for the region. Everyday I walked around in bitter, freezing cold, ice, snow, sleet and rain. I peered through cracks and holes of locked and enclosed T-hangars (small T shaped hangars that house the smaller airplanes) and large hangars, hoping to spot an N-number. Often, the airplanes in the T-hangars were in total darkness. As I peered into these hangars, an occasional ray of light would penetrate a hole or crack in a wall or door of a hangar. Many times, these holes or cracks allowed for just enough light so as to reveal the N-number on the side of the airplane. I looked for every N-number I could find. I often wanted to change places with many of the airplanes. They were much more warm and dry than I was. In spite of the weather, I plowed forward. I went everywhere in that airport, recording N-numbers.

At the end of four weeks, I had accumulated ten pages of N-numbers (about 3,000) . Now, at that stage all I had to do was go to the FAA office and look up each and every N-number on microfilm. Beginning on a Monday and ending on the following Friday, I spent eight hours a day at the microfilm looking up N-numbers. It was exhausting work. However, what really made the job tough was my *fear*. By this stage, hopelessness seemed to knock on my door everyday during that time. I heard thoughts and voices saying things like:

*"You have spent weeks at this and don't have a dollar to show for it."*

*"What if this doesn't work?"*

*"Look at all of the time you are spending writing down N-numbers."*

*"What makes you think you will ever see one dollar from all of this work?"*

*"Look at all of the time you are spending in this FAA office."*

*"These people (the ones in the FAA office) think you are crazy."*

*"This will never produce any money."*

*"What will your wife and children do for food?"*

*"Why are you doing this?"*

*"You are a failure."*

*"You are going to fall flat on your face."*

*"Look at what you are doing to your family."*

*"This is not and will not produce any income."*
*"You are only fooling yourself."*

These voices and thoughts were very real within my being. They made me want to quit and give up. What if just one of these feelings or fears held out to be true, much less several of them?

I remember going to the airport with a knot in my stomach *everyday*. Everyday was a *risk*. Could I afford to *risk* going forward with this business, with the *real* possibility that it would *never* produce one dime?

The thoughts and doubting voices constantly riddled my being. It seemed as though every step I took was like having to walk through several feet of thick mud.

Finally, I came to the point where I decided that, yes, I may very well die, fail and/or ruin my family. Regardless of what the outcome would be, though, I was going to continue and not stop or quit for anything. The whole thing would have to fall flat on its face for me to quit.

With this decision, a greater resolve came into my being. This resolve did *not* remove the knots from my stomach nor the fear I felt in the face of the risks of failure vs. success (I lost over twenty pounds during those weeks). However, the decision to risk it all and remain committed to the end helped me to carry on from day-to-day, despite the negative, debilitating feelings and fears.

Ultimately, through my efforts with the N-numbers, I acquired the names of the owners of over 1,000 aircraft hangared or tied down at the airport. Within a matter of weeks, I was servicing my first customers, washing my first airplanes. My pitfalls did not end with the N-numbers, however. I continued to experience several more barriers. Each one confronted me as a major risk of failure. During the first six months of this business, it seemed as if I was having to climb a major mountain every day. With each mountain, I faced a major dilemma and decision:

*"Should I choose to plow forward and run the risk*
*of failure,*

*or*

*should I stop while it is still emotionally safe,*
*and just get a job?"*

I chose to face each dilemma head on, with a knotted stomach and full of fear. I faced each problem, one at a time. Ultimately, I was successful.

In the end, many months later, I was able to successfully sell the business and move my family to Texas where I resumed and completed my graduate education and further developed our counseling/life-improvement process.

Since that time, I have learned that all of life is much like what I met with daily at that airport. You and I are always confronted with choices.

Do we take the risk or do we do what is comfortable, *emotionally*?

Do we risk being rejected and enter into a *relationship* with someone we are attracted to? Or do we keep to ourselves because it is more comfortable than having to go through the fear of rejection?

Do we take the *business* risk and hope to experience the desired success? Or, do we go for the sure thing and remain in our *emotional* comfort zone?

The problem for many of us is that when we choose the comfort zone we become very embittered as we grow older. We spend our later years in the "would-a, should-a, could-a" mind-set. We go to our graves with internal regrets over some of the choices we made during the span of our lives. However, life does not have to be this way—if we will live a life of *faith*, or *emotional* risk-taking.

**What is Faith?**

Faith is to your *emotional*-self what risk-taking is to your physical-self. Faith is much more than a religious trust or belief in an unseen Creator. In its truest form, faith is emotional *risk-taking*. It is the ability to take risks. Faith is: *believing that something you can not see will happen or occur.*

Oddly enough, fear and faith both have this definition.

However, even though faith and fear have the same definition, they produce two opposite results in our lives. Fear, as we have seen, produces doubt, second-guessing, paralyzation and fright. Faith, on the other hand, produces confidence, optimism and greater feelings of faith—risk-taking!

### Hope Produces Faith

When you are feeling and experiencing feelings of hope (Chapter Sixteen), you feel and experience greater amounts of optimism. This, in turn, triggers the desire and motivation to take risks. You feel an ability to believe, trust and hold to a faith (or ability to risk) that the outcome (of your choice or decision) will ultimately work out in your favor, whether it is with a relationship or a venture. Feelings of faith will express themselves and manifest themselves in varied ways. You may feel faith in your Creator, yourself, your abilities, your instincts, your friends or the forces of nature. However the faith is displayed, it is resident within your *emotional*-self. Emotionally, you feel and experience "*faith*."

So, the whole, complete, healed you, your *real*-self, will feel and experience feelings of *holiness*.

Holiness, in turn, triggers or produces feelings of *hope*.

Hope, in turn, triggers or produces felt emotions of *faith*, or emotional risk-taking (see Illus. 17–1).

Once faith is firmly rooted and entrenched within your heart, it too will produce a natural fruit. We learn of this fruit in the next chapter. This subsequent by-product, or fruit, which springs from faith, in my opinion, is the most powerful and dynamic emotional experience you can have. Every good and positive aspect and experience of life comes from the presence of this one emotion. However, the absence of this one emotion is also at the core of so many of the negative, destructive realities in our lives, our homes and our society.

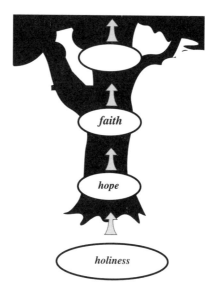

Illus. 17–1: **Faith: The Trunk**

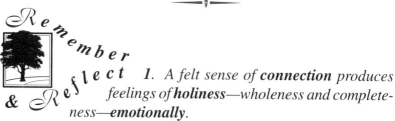

**1.** *A felt sense of **connection** produces feelings of **holiness**—wholeness and completeness—**emotionally**.*

**2.** *Holiness produces **hope**.*

**3.** *Hope produces **faith**.*

**4.** *Faith is more than trust or belief. It is **risk-taking**. It can only come if you **first** feel hope, which is an **internal** emotional feeling of **optimism** that you feel toward yourself and your life.*

**5.** *This process is emotional, not physical, mental or spiritual. However, it almost always affects the mental, physical and spiritual areas of your life. It is an emotional process that controls your feelings and attitudes. These feelings and attitudes, repeatedly felt and experienced often enough, eventually become behavioral habits.*

# CHAPTER 18

# *Love: The Trunk*
## *The Other Side of Life*

*"There are three things that remain — <u>faith</u>, <u>hope</u>, and <u>love</u> — and the greatest of these is <u>love</u>."*

**The Bible**

*I*f you and I approach a crowd and ask for a definition of love, we will get a multitude of answers. One person will respond by saying that love is a *feeling*. Yet another might answer that love is *acceptance*. Another will say that love is *God*. Yet someone else will probably say that love is a *commitment*. The thought of love being only a commitment seems so dry, doesn't it?

We talk about love. We sing about love. We write books about love. We write books about being *in* love. We watch television shows about love. We are lured to love. Yet, we can not adequately define or explain love.

When it comes to defining love, we stumble. Love is hard to conceptualize. However, most of us are quickly aware of its presence when it is around us. Likewise, we are also painfully aware of its absence. We know we need love. Often, however, we find it difficult to explain love.

Love's existence, or the lack of its existence, is always around us. In the absence of love, fear prevails. Our reaction to fear is self-preservation, aggression and even defiant rebellion. Our world's history, at times, seems to reflect more of a lack of love than it does the presence of love. With love, there would be no wars, no fighting, no violence, no thievery. With love, our court and legal system might shrink. With love, spirits relax, fears subside and hearts become calm. Love motivates us to open up and be vulnerable: mentally, emotionally, physically and spiritually. The power of love is enormous. Yet, we can not communicably define or explain love in simple, easy-to-understand terms. The definitions we attempt always seem to limit and leave short the real essence of love.

Pondering this age-old dilemma reminds me of a client we worked with last year. I will refer to him as Walter. Walter was a man who had an incredibly strong felt sense of connection with his Creator. In spite of this, fear, rejection and self-preservation constantly plagued Walter's life. He lived his life feeling and fearing rejection. Because of this he experienced a lot of rejection. He often brought it into the room with himself, unknowingly of course. His fear of rejection and self-preservation caused great difficulty in every relationship in his life: his marriage, a couple of close friends, even his work relationships — primarily with his bosses.

Seeing Walter's dilemma, we gave him a simple assignment:

"Compile a list of every time in your life when you can remember *feeling* love."

This is a fairly simple and typical assignment in our counseling/life improvement process. With this assignment completed, we knew we would be able to replicate the triggers that produced feelings of love within Walter—which was one item he was needing for his own healing.

When Walter returned for his next session the following week, we were heart-stricken with his completed assignment. As it turned out Walter could only remember *one* time in his life when he felt love. One! The circumstances surrounding that one event will probably remain in my mind forever.

Walter grew up in a physically loving environment. That is, his parents provided the physical necessities for him. They saw to it that Walter never did without, physically or materially. But mentally and emotionally, it was a completely different story. Walter grew up around continual verbal abuse. His father often cursed him and cursed at him. When I say often, I mean often— as in all of the time, as a regular conversational pattern. It was not uncommon for Walter to be called or referred to as a "bastard" or "little s.o.b." I was horrified as I heard of the names Walter had endured at the hands of his father. He heard himself being characterized in this way throughout his childhood and teen years.

When Walter was old enough, he moved away from home. His one experience with love came during this time in his life. Walter had been living on his own for about two years. He was studying to be a minister. As with most college students who are on their own, money was tight. To make his dollars stretch, Walter rented a room in the home of a couple who attended his church.

Because of the intense emotional pain he had experienced for most of his life, Walter had little contact with his family. It was not that he hated them or rejected them. He was simply unable to emotionally deal with or handle their verbal onslaughts every time they would talk or meet.

At this point you may be thinking, "This Walter guy surely must have done or said things to bring a lot of this on himself?" We thought this may be a possibility at first. Yet, as we probed the situation, we discovered that this was not so. Walter's father was an alcoholic. He was also very physically abusive to Walter's mother. From what we gathered, no one ever stood up to the man and his behavior. Everyone, out of fear, accommodated the father's behavior.

After living, studying and working around the people in Walter's parish or church congregation, everyone, including Walter's minister and Walter's landlords, knew Walter very well.

They liked him a lot, too. Walter was a very likable fellow. Because of his own childhood experiences, he grew to have a very tender, caring and compassionate heart. He was readily able to feel for and understand the pains, difficulties and struggles of others around him. Because of this he demonstrated this caring heart toward all of those around him. Yet, with this, he still battled fear, rejection and self-preservation.

One evening, while in college, Walter received a telephone call from his father. His parents were wanting to know when he would be coming to visit them. Because of the years of emotional pain at the hands of his family environment, Walter had pretty much stayed away from his family during those first two years that he was out on his own.

His parent's request soon became a violent verbal attack. Within minutes, Walter's father was tearing Walter to shreds, verbally. Walter's father accused Walter of being ungrateful, non-caring and disrespectful. But his father used language far more severe than I am using here. Walter's father attacked Walter's faith and questioned its validity. Before too long into the conversation, Walter was in tears. His pain, which he had worked so hard to overcome during the previous two years, had thrust itself upon him, with a full force. In internal torment and pain, Walter hung up the phone on his father. Doing this made him feel even more disrespectful and inconsiderate. It compounded his negative feelings and made him feel guilty. It made him feel that some of his father's accusations could be correct.

Being emotionally overcome, Walter quickly left the house and took a walk. A flood of tears accompanied Walter on his walk. His emotional pain was enormous.

While Walter was on his walk, his father called back. With Walter away, his landlord answered the phone. Since Walter's father could not unload on Walter, he unloaded on Walter's landlord. Before he knew it, Walter's landlord was hearing a cutting, violent language, the likes of which he had never heard before in his life (he was an elderly man who had lived a long life). Walter's father went on to refer to Walter by every name in the book. The landlord was horrified.

After several minutes of listening to the father's verbal attacks of Walter, Walter's landlord interrupted Walter's father by saying,

*"Mister, I do not know who you are talking about. But you are not referring to the young man who lives with us in our home."*

With this, the phone conversation soon ended. Walter was on his walk while this phone conversation took place and was unaware that his father had called again.

After walking for about an hour (it took that much time for him to be able to stop the crying), Walter returned to his room. While sitting in a chair in his room, Walter's landlord knocked on his door. Still working on his composure, Walter invited his landlord to enter his room. The landlord opened the door. Walter could tell something was wrong, terribly wrong. His landlord's countenance was as that of grief and death. He felt something bad was about to happen to him. He was sure of it. This is what he had grown accustomed to while growing up in his own home.

Standing at Walter's door, his landlord began,

*"Walter, while you were out, your father called."*

With this, Walter lost what little composure he had gathered. His tears and pain resurfaced. Walter was now expecting to hear words of rejection and condemnation. The landlord continued,

*"Walter, your father said some things and used some language that I frankly have never heard before. He said most of them in reference to you. I honestly, in all my years, have never heard a parent say the kind of things about his own child that I heard your father say about you tonight. I can not see how a parent could say those kinds of things about his own child.*

*I just want you to know that I told your father that with all intended respect to him, I did not know the person he was referring to. I told your father that the young man staying in our home is not the person he was referring to.*

*Walter, I want you to know, that regardless of what is going on between you and your father, I believe in you."*

Having said this, Walter's landlord left the room. Walter cried the night away. It was with those words from his landlord that Walter first felt unconditional love from another person. Walter's landlord had affirmed his belief in Walter. He poured an unconditional gift into Walter's heart. *This* had been Walter's *one* experience with love.

With this, we began a Journey with Walter that caused him to feel, experience and encounter more of this love. In time, his wounds healed and his preoccupation with fear, rejection and self-preservation subsided. For Walter, love was acceptance.

### Faith Produces Love

Once faith is firmly seeded or "rooted" within your heart, or *emotional*-self, it also triggers or produces a natural "fruit" or reaction. The "fruit" of faith is *love* (see Illus 18–1).

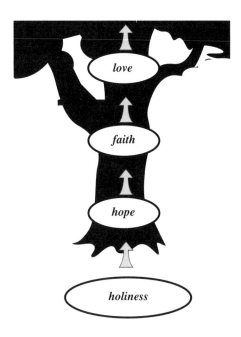

Illus. 18–1: **Love: The Trunk**

A willingness to take risks and to be vulnerable (mentally, emotionally, physically, relationally, vocationally and spiritually) often results in greater feelings of love. All too often, we do not take risks because we fear the consequences of the risk. But, often our fear is based on our past experiences with wounding, not risk-taking. This behavior short-circuits all opportunities to feel and experience genuine love. In order to feel and experience authentic, emotional love, you have to take risks. You can not have an apple without an apple seed. Neither can you have or experience love without faith: being open, transparent, vulnerable and taking risks. Vulnerability is the seed and love is the fruit.

As your faith, or risk-taking, works out in your favor, you feel greater amounts of love. You feel loved and affirmed by your Creator, by others and/or even by yourself. Love floods your entire being after you have successfully exercised risk-taking. Notice we did not say *experience* risk? It is in *exercising*, not experiencing, emotional risk-taking, that you ultimately will experience success. These subsequent experiences cause you to feel very loved and affirmed.

Love is the purest, natural high. Experiencing love causes you to give love. When you receive and experience so much love, your natural inclination is to emit some of what you are filled with—love.

At this stage in the emotional progression, this dynamic power changes your entire being. It takes over your consciousness and forever changes your life. This is because of the power contained within the feelings of love. Love can be the greatest energy force within your *emotional*-self. Love has the power to heal and it has the power to set you free—mentally, physically, spiritually and emotionally. Love has the power to cause you to change your direction or course in life. When love is firmly in place as a felt emotion, it affects and influences what you *do*, what you *say*, what you *think*, and what you *feel*. Love is powerful.

**Love Conquers Fear**

Many people believe that fear is probably the greatest emotion one can experience. When you think about it, this idea certainly seems reasonable. Fear alters everyone's behavior, doesn't it? Fear will cause you to do, say, think and feel things that are not even real. Yet, because the fear *feels* real, you abide by the impression it stamps on your heart and mind. We work with many people who come to us because they can not control their fear; it controls them.

So, how do we conquer fear? What can we do to be free from the clutches of fear? The answer comes, again, from the Bible:

*"Perfect love casts out all fear."*
**The Bible**

What does this mean? It means that the level of felt fear which you experience at any given moment within your *emotional*-self, is in *direct proportion* to the level of love that occupies your *emotional*-self. In other words, when a high level of fear exists within you, it is because there is a correspondingly *low* level of felt love within your *emotional*-self. Likewise, when there is a high level of love existing within your heart, there will be lower levels of fear.

We work this principle to the hilt within our counseling/life-improvement process. When an individual is firmly entrenched in fear, we assign projects and assignments for them that we know, when performed, will *trigger* and *cause* the client to *feel* greater measures of love, emotionally. Because of the cause-and-effect system of order within all of us, we know that when we are feeling greater measures of love, the controlling power of fear diminishes within our lives.

You may be thinking, *"It can not be that easy."*

All I can say to that skepticism is that it works every time, without fail, like clockwork. It works, however, not because of some magical assignment or process that we have developed. It works so effectively because it revolves around a basic law or principle of the emotional realm:

*"Perfect love casts out all fear."*

Once you or I, or anyone else, is feeling greater measures of love, fear subsides. It does not necessarily go away. However, the fear subsides radically enough so that we can get a handle on our thoughts, our feelings and our lives.

### Where Does Love Come From?

As we learned in Chapter Fifteen, love is triggered by felt emotions of *connection*. Connection produces love. Connection is love. Love is not passive or defensive. It requires risk and vulnerability. Such action takes strength, not weakness. Love is assertive. Love is aggressive. It requires much more strength to be open, transparent and vulnerable than it does to build a shell and project a front of strength.

In the absence of love and connection, wounding prevails. Barricaded or barriered resistance hinders love—both love coming in and love going out.

### What is Love?

Love is the feeling of *unwarranted and unconditional giving and acceptance.* Love is more than a feeling of "being in love." It is also much more than feeling "loved." It is much more than sex. It is much more than romance. We are not diminishing these qualities, not at all. However, to limit love to one or two of these qualities is to limit life and emotional experience. Love is far more than all of these qualities put together. Love is *feeling* and *receiving* unwarranted and unconditional gifts of giving and acceptance from your Creator and from others. Love is also *giving* unwarranted and unconditional gifts of giving and acceptance into the lives of others around you. Most of us seek to experience the former half of the description of love: *"feeling and receiving."*

However, oddly enough it is the latter aspect of love, *"giv-ing,"* that causes a far greater process of healing within an individual.

### Giving Love Produces Personal Healing and Change

Giving love produces personal healing and change. We know this to be fact because we have worked with it for years. Often when an individual is entrenched in their wounded, negative or fearful nature, it is not the *getting* of love that turns them around toward healing and change. What often pulls us out of our pit, and turns us toward genuine healing and change, are our own acts and words of *giving* love. This, too, works without fail within the *emotional*-self. Isn't this interesting? I do not fully understand it. However, I know that it works with great predictability.

In its rawest, purest form, love is *unconditional giving and unconditional acceptance.*

The giving can be a *word*, or an *action*, or a physical *gift*. The giving can even be a *thought* that you choose to believe and dwell on with regard to others. Whatever the channel for expressing the giving may be, love is unconditional *giving*. This attitude and life style of giving is directed toward yourself, your Creator, your life, or toward others around you.

The important thing to realize is that love — *unconditional giving and unconditional acceptance*—is not merely some act. It is a *feeling* and an *attitude*. Frankly, love is much, much more of a feeling and attitude than it is an *act* or a *word*. The acts and words should be a small *evidence* of the deeply resident love felt and abiding within you or me.

The interesting thing about love is that once you are feeling and experiencing its true essence, love produces more love. It propagates faster than rabbits. The reproductive effect that love has on the heart is tremendous. This is why it is the most powerful emotional expression *and* experience known to man. This is why it has the ability to heal, to change and to alter every facet of your being, for the better. This is why love has the ability to alter every facet of our entire society and world.

Once this power is flooding, flowing and controlling your being, it causes and triggers feelings, motivations and desires like this:

*"Love is very patient and kind, never jealous or envious, never boastful or proud, never haughty or selfish or rude. Love does not demand its own way. It is not irritable or touchy. It does not hold grudges and will hardly even notice when others do it wrong. It is never glad about injustice, but rejoices whenever truth wins out. If you love someone you will be loyal to him no matter what the cost. You will always believe in him, and always stand your ground in defending him. All of the special gifts and powers from God will someday come to an end, but love goes on forever."*
**The Bible**

This is the kind of effect that love can have on you and me. Isn't that incredible? It is powerful. Once you are touched by pure, unconditional love, your life is forever changed. Our greatest quest in life should be the pursuit and attainment of this emotional experience of love.

However, it can only be found if and when you are first feeling and experiencing feelings of *holiness*—wholeness, completeness—*emotionally*, through a felt sense of *connection*. This, in turn, will trigger feelings of *hope*, which then will trigger feelings of *faith* (optimism and risk-taking). It is at this point in the internal emotional process that you or I can feel and experience genuine *love*, *receiving* love and *giving* love—unconditional giving and acceptance.

Once your *emotional*-self is at this stage, love will manifest itself through three distinct channels, or "branches." Each of these three "branches" relate to your relationship with,

*yourself,*
*others* around you and
*your Creator.*
This will be covered beginning with the next chapter.

———¶———

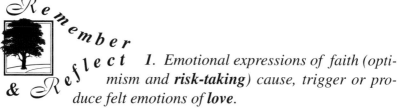

1. *Emotional expressions of faith (opti-mism and* **risk-taking**) *cause, trigger or pro-duce felt emotions of* **love**.
2. *Love is powerful enough to conquer and control fear.*
3. *Love is* **unconditional giving** *and* **unconditional acceptanc**e.
4. *Love is an* **emotion** *and an* **attitude**. *It is not merely an action. Actions and words of love are fruits of genuine, felt love living within the heart.*

# CHAPTER 19

# *Whole, Healed Outward Behavior:*
# *The Fruit*
### *The Other Side of Life*

*"For if the roots of the tree are holy, the branches will be too."*
**The Bible**

$\mathcal{J}$ust as your wounded-self produces wounded outward behavior, so also your *real*-self, the whole and healed you, produces outward behavior, or "fruit." From Chapter Ten we learned that our wounded outward behavior is branched through three realms of relationship within each of our lives. The same is true for the outward behavior of the *real*-self.

As we walk in love, healing, freedom and peace we find that our heart is manifesting or producing outward behavior that directly influences our relationships toward ourselves, our friends and our Creator. But, what are those outward behaviors? What are those "fruits"? Each of these three "branches," or areas of relationships, within our lives produces at least three emotional qualities (see Illus. 19:1). All of these emotions are the result of feeling and experiencing a felt sense of holiness within the core of our *emotional*-self. The emotional "fruits" of a whole, healed

Illus. 19–1: **The Fruits of the Real-Self**

self are: peace, patience, self-control, love, gentleness, kindness, faithfulness, joy and goodness.

Do you notice anything significant about this list? These are the qualities we first mentioned in Chapter Seven. They are the qualities listed in the Bible, from a section titled Galatians, known as "The Fruits of the Spirit."

The Bible teaches its readers that these qualities are characteristics that God's children should possess. For centuries people have attempted to acquire or wear these qualities like one would wear a suit of clothes. However, such attempts have always ended in failure. Why? Because, the *emotional*-self is a multi-level, multi-tiered entity (Chapter Seven). Consequently, like a tree, our *emotional*-self produces feelings and emotions that come from deeper, inward "root" feelings, emotions and experiences.

Now we can begin to see why we often fail when we try to put these qualities on ourselves like a suit of clothes. These qualities can only be produced from *within* once the "root" of holiness exists within our *emotional*-self. We can not *acquire* these "fruits."

These emotional "fruits" are *not* experienced by attempting to focus on any other aspect of our *emotional*-self (other emotions that are progressively beyond the "root" or starting point, such as those in the trunk, branches, or fruit). We have to focus our energy on feeling and experiencing the "root" *of holiness—* wholeness and completeness— *emotionally*. This then, will ultimately produce the external "fruits" or feelings of peace, patience, self-control, love, gentleness, kindness, faithfulness, joy and goodness.

We will explore *how* these nine "fruits" are produced as outward behavior in the next three chapters.

———— ❧ ————

*Remember & Reflect*

1. *Just as the wounded-self produces outward behavior, or "fruit," so also, the **real**-self produces "fruit."*

2. *The "fruit" of the **real**-self is peace, patience, self-control, love, gentleness, kindness, faithfulness, joy and goodness.*

3. *These nine emotional qualities are "branched" or channeled through three basic areas, or realms of relationship in each of our lives.*

# CHAPTER 20

# *Responsibility:*
# *The First Branch*
## *The Other Side of Life*

*But when the Holy Spirit controls our lives He will produce this kind of fruit in us: <u>peace</u>, <u>patience</u>, <u>self-control</u> . . ."*

**The Bible**

$\mathcal{B}$y way of reminder, it is important to remember that the emotional progression, or chain reaction, that we have discussed throughout the previous chapters is *emotional*. It is not mental (psychological), spiritual or physical. This is an *emotional* process that occurs within your *emotional*-self. Because of the power of the *emotional*-self, these feelings and emotions will affect and have a measured determination on your mental, spiritual and physical beings, as well. This chain-reaction effect occurs within you whether you are experiencing emotions from a wounded nature or from a healed nature.

Once your healed-self, or *real*-self has progressed to the stage of love, your *emotional*-self will channel your feelings and emotions through three distinct and different channels, or "branches":
Responsibility,
Respect and
Reverence.

These three "branches" are each related to and connected with the three realms of relationship in your life:

relationship with yourself,

relationship with others around you and

relationship with your Creator and the spirit realm.

### Responsibility

The first branch through which love channels itself is "Responsibility" (see Illus. 20–1). This branch affects your relationship with yourself and produces the fruits of peace, patience and self control.

When the *emotional*-self is free of wounding, pain, fear, depression and anger, it is free to experience love. It is free to receive love. It is free to give love. As this is taking place within your heart or *emotional*-self, you find that you have a greater motivation to be in charge, in control and responsible for:

*who you are,*

*how you feel, and for*

*the circumstances in your life.*

As a matter of fact, when in this focus, you guard this religiously. You do not want to give up this emotional control. Why? Because you know that to do so is *emotional* suicide. Giving up emotional control places you in a very weak and emotionally vulnerable position. It sets you up for wounding, pain, depression, anger and fear.

Our human nature will always work against being responsible and in control. Why? Because our human nature is always wanting what it perceives as the easy and comfortable way out. However, as we learned from Chapter Ten, when you or I look to "emotional saviors" or attempt to "return to the womb" emotionally, we are only setting ourselves up for greater disaster, *emotionally*. The price we pay for an illusion of false comfort is not really worth it.

Illus. 20–1: **Responsibility: The First Branch**

So, as love becomes a felt expression within our hearts, we willfully determine to be responsible for, and in control of, our life. Our Creator has given us the power and ability to take this control. Through love, we must possess it and live in it.

### Counting the Costs and Fitting In

In this position we take great measure to "count the costs" with regard to any given decision, relationship, venture or activity. Why? Because we know that when we are responsible, after everything is said and done, the buck stops with each of us and our own decisions. We can not blame experiences, other people, or even God, when we choose to take responsibility for our own feelings. So, we "count the cost."

In so doing, we are far more likely to experience greater success in every relationship, decision, venture or activity. How so? Because when we "count the cost," we know ahead of time what the probable outcome or outcomes may be. Consequently, we are *better prepared* for each possible outcome that may follow our choice or decision.

With this approach, we are far more likely to choose only those relationships, business ventures and activities that have a greater degree of being able to *fit us* and our heart-nature. We will not worry about "*fitting in*." We will seek avenues that *fit us*.

When we live life irresponsibly, the opposite is true. We make choices hoping we will "fit in" (versus asking if it fits us), hoping that, in the end, things will work out. Usually, it does *not* work out as we had hoped. This then usually triggers hurt, wounding, pain, disappointment, rejection and frustration. When this happens, we then blame everything and everyone else for our feelings and predicament, being blinded to the fact that *we* made the decisions that set us up for these problems in the first place. No one else made these decisions. Yet, we blame others, just the same. It is almost as if we fear to admit failure.

When taking responsibility, most of us usually have a very good idea, *beforehand*, whether or not things will be a fit or work to our desired outcome. Again, this is because we have counted the costs *ahead of time*. We have a good notion as to whether or not the intended decision fits our heart nature.

Also, with this mode of emotional living, the chances of becoming overwhelmed by depression and depressive behavior are almost nonexistent. We say "almost" simply because even in our best attempts to be in control and responsible there are still times when, in spite of our best efforts, events occur that truly are beyond our control. However, this is usually less than a ten percent factor if we are taking all of the proper measures with our decision-making, counting the costs ahead of time. These "proper measures" flow naturally when we are living in a mode of personal responsibility, emotionally.

### The Fruit, or Outward Emotional Behavior

Once love is channeling itself through the avenue or "branch" of personal emotional *responsibility*, it culminates its journey within your *emotional*-self through *external emotional behavior and feelings*. These outward emotional behaviors and feelings are:

*peace*,
*patience*, and
*self-control* (see Illus. 20–2).

The external feelings (peace, patience and self-control), and the behaviors they produce, directly relate to your relationship toward yourself. In other words, as your emotions freely flow through all levels of your *emotional*-self, they ultimately culminate through your outward, external behavior. This facet or "branch" of your emotional behavior relates to your relationship with yourself. These three "fruits" are all *felt emotions* that you experience toward *yourself*. That is, when you take personal emotional responsibility, you will experience:

greater measures of inner *peace*,
greater measures of *patience*, and
greater measures of *self-control*, within yourself and toward yourself.

** Each of these emotional qualities directly relates to and affects your relationship and attitude toward *yourself*.

### What are Peace, Patience and Self-control?

Each of these three qualities is a felt emotion within your *emotional*-self. Specifically though, how can you be aware of their presence or existence within your heart and life? To answer this question, you simply need to know and be aware of what these three "fruits" feel like when they are flowing in and through your *emotional*-self.

**1.** *Peace* is an internal *restful contentment and pleasure* that you feel toward yourself and toward your life.

**2.** *Patience* is an internal *willingness to restfully wait.* With it you have the feeling that everything is fine and OK; you are on schedule, there is no panic in Heaven, only plans. Your Creator has this thing called life under control. So, you relax toward the matters at hand.

**3.** *Self-control* is an internal *desire and motivation to harness, channel and direct your words, actions and thoughts.*

Each of these three "fruits" is produced *effortlessly* and *naturally* from <u>within</u> your *emotional*-self when you are whole, healed, free and at peace, *and* when you are feeling and experiencing a deep sense of holiness—wholeness and completeness—within your life. These three "fruits" are a result of the *natural* emotional flow that culminates and manifests itself in your feelings and attitude toward yourself.

So, now can you see why we often fail when we try to acquire or wear these qualities like a suit of clothes? These qualities are produced from *within* because of the underlying *root* within us. We can not acquire these "fruits." We can only *produce* them, once we have the "root" of emotional *holiness*— wholeness and completeness—*emotionally.*

Can you now see why, in order to feel and experience inner peace, or patience, or self-control, you have to begin by addressing the root: the feelings of holiness or the lack thereof? These emotional "fruits" or external qualities can not be experienced by attempting to focus on any other aspect of your *emotional*-self (emotions that are progressively beyond the root or starting point, such as love, faith or hope, which are in the trunk). You have to focus your energy on feeling and experiencing the root of

*peace,*
*patience,*
*self-control*
**************
fruits of the spirit

responsibility

love

faith

hope

holiness

Illus. 20–2: **Peace, Patience, Self-Control: The Fruit**

*holiness*—wholeness and completeness—*emotionally*. This will then ultimately produce the positive and pleasurable external emotional "fruits" which you want and desire.

*Remember & Reflect*  *1. The whole and healed **emotional**-self, once progressed to the stage of love, will manifest itself through three "branches," all of which spawn outward behavior, or "fruits."*

2. *The first "branch" is "**Responsibility**," personally.*
3. *This "branch" is directed toward **yourself**.*
4. *These feelings of "Responsibility" exist because you are in control and in charge of who you are, how you feel and for the circumstances in your life.*
5. *This "branch" of emotional responsibility always produces outward behaviors or "fruits" that, when left to themselves, will produce feelings and behavior of **peace**, **patience** and **self-control**.*
6. *When left unbridled and uncontrolled, this emotional "fruit" inevitably builds and enhances healthy self-confidence, self-esteem and self-value. It produces self-affirmed living, not self-focused or selfish living.*

# CHAPTER 21

# *Respect:*
# *The Second Branch*
## *The Other Side of Life*

*"But when the Holy Spirit controls our lives He will produce this kind of fruit in us: . . . love, gentleness, kindness . . ."*

**The Bible**

*T*he second avenue through which love will channel itself is "Respect" (see Illus 21–1). This "branch" affects your relationship with *others* around you. It relates to your ability to respect and trust others.

### Pleasurable Relationships

When your *emotional*-self is free of wounding, pain, fear, depression and anger, it is free to *experience love*. It is free to receive love. It is free to give love. As this is taking place within your heart or *emotional*-self, you find that you have a *deep rest-fulness* toward the relationships around you. A *peaceful trust* replaces what used to be a mistrust toward the very people you once feared would hurt you or let you down.

In this mode, relationships are comfortable for you. You feel much more relaxed and at peace with your friends, your family

Illus. 21–1:  **Respect: The Second Branch**

and your loved ones.  Fear of further wounding no longer haunts your heart.  How can this be?  It happens because you are *free* to receive and give love.  As you are experiencing love, you naturally desire to let your own love flow into the lives of those around you, acquaintances and even strangers.  You develop a life style of loving people and giving love into people.

### Understanding Replaces a Desire to be Understood.

When you are in this state of being, you grow into a heightened awareness of the feelings and emotions of others around you. You now have the ability to understand the feelings, fears, wounds and circumstances of many of those surrounding your life. *Understanding replaces the desire to be understood.* Where you once were consumed with the desire to be understood, you now have the ability to live a life of understanding others. You now are able to *feel* for them. Consequently, your compassion, tenderness, love and mercy for others increases. In short, you become a clearer reflection of the Creator who formed you. At this point, you are reflecting "His Image" into the lives of those around you.

Invariably, this transformation draws those around you to you and to your Creator. Why? Because everyone is starving for the feeling of being understood. Everyone is starving for the feelings of freedom from their hurt and wounding. Everyone desires the feeling of peace. Everyone desires love. Consequently, your loving nature draws people to you. As you dispense love and hope into others' lives, this in turn, draws them closer to their Creator.

You may fear that this activity will draw other people to you in an unhealthy fashion. You may fear that an unhealthy emotional dependence is developing. This is not true. Unhealthy emotional dependencies develop when two people are *both* emotionally unhealthy, imbalanced and wounded. One of these two will project and portray himself or herself to be the opposite of this. He or she projects an air of healthiness, wholeness and maturity. This projection draws the other wounded, hurting person to them in an unhealthy dependence. Ultimately, the wounding and neediness of each of them causes both parties to feed off of one another. This unhealthy relationship destroys many who are in its path.

One who is genuinely whole, healed, free and at peace will *not* allow this activity to occur. By instinct and by decision, the healed individual wants to draw the wounded individual into wholeness, healing, freedom, peace and love, not into an unhealthy dependence. This can only occur as the wounded individual links up *emotionally* with his or her Creator and experiences genuine and permanent healing, freedom, peace and love—*emotionally*. The healed person knows this and abides in it.

### The Fruit, or Outward Emotional Behavior

Once love is channeling itself through the avenue or "branch" of *respect*, it culminates its journey within your *emotional*-self through *external emotional behavior and feelings*. These outward emotional behaviors and feelings are:

*love*,

*gentleness, and*

*kindness* (see Illus. 21–2).

In other words, as your emotions freely flow through all levels of your *emotional*-self, they ultimately culminate through your outward, external behavior. These external feelings and behaviors are *love*, *gentleness* and *kindness*. Notice that these three "fruits" are all felt emotions that you experience and express toward other people in your life. That is, when you experience a healthy respect toward others, you will experience:

greater measures of *love*,

greater measures of *gentleness*, and

greater measures of *kindness*, toward others in your life.

** Each of these emotional qualities directly relates to and affects your relationship with *others around you.*

### What are Love, Gentleness and Kindness?

Each of these three qualities is a felt emotion within your *emotional*-self. Specifically, though, how can you be aware of their presence within your heart and life? To answer this question, you simply need to know and be aware of what these three "fruits" feel like when they are flowing in and through your *emotional*-self.

**1.** *Love* is a heart of *unconditional giving and acceptance* toward life and others. However, it is not only giving in to the lives of others; it is also the ability to *receive* the unconditional,

Illus. 21–2: **Love, Gentleness, Kindness: The Fruit**

unwarranted gifts and kindnesses of others, including your Creator.

**2.** *Gentleness* is a soft, tender, *compassion* toward those around you. It carries with it an *understanding* for the circumstances in which others may find themselves.

**3.** *Kindness* is an open willingness to *accept others* for *who they are* and *where they are* in life (emotionally, mentally, spiritually and physically), much as your Creator accepts them. This does not necessarily mean that you choose to live with or tolerate their ways; it means that you accept them. There is a big difference between the two.

When you are whole, healed, free and at peace, *and* when you are feeling and experiencing a deep sense of *connection* in your life, your *emotional*-self produces each of these three emotions *effortlessly* and *naturally*. These three "fruits" are the *natural* emotional flow that manifests itself in your feelings and attitude toward others around you.

So, now can you begin to see why we often fail when we try to put these qualities on ourselves like a suit of clothes? These qualities are produced from *within* because of the underlying *root* within us. We can not acquire these "fruits." We can only *produce* them, once we have the "root" of *holiness*—wholeness and completeness—*emotionally*.

In order to feel and experience inner love, gentleness and kindness toward others in your life, you have to begin by addressing the "root" or feelings of *holiness*. These emotional "fruits" or external emotional qualities are not experienced by attempting to focus on any other aspect of your *emotional*-self (emotions that are progressively beyond the root or starting point, such as hope, faith or love, which are in the trunk). You must focus your energy on feeling and experiencing *holiness*—wholeness and completeness—*emotionally*. This will then ultimately produce the positive and pleasurable external emotional "fruits" which you want and desire.

*Remember & Reflect*

1. *The whole and healed* **emotional**-*self, your* **real**-*self, once progressed to the stage of love, will manifest itself through three "branches," all of which spawn outward behaviors, or "fruits."*

2. *The second "branch" is "Respect," toward* **others**.

3. *This "branch" affects your relationship with others around you.*

4. *These feelings of "Respect" exist because of felt emotions of* **love**, *which trigger an ability to* **trust** *others.*

5. *This "branch" of emotional* **respect** *always produces outward behavior or "fruits" that, when left to themselves, will produce feelings and behavior of* **love**, **gentleness** *and* **kindness**.

6. *When left unbridled and uncontrolled, this emotional "fruit" inevitably builds and enhances healthy, successful friendships and relationships.*

# CHAPTER 22

# Reverence:
# The Third Branch
### The Other Side of Life

*"But when the Holy Spirit controls our lives He will produce this kind of fruit in us: ... <u>faithfulness</u>, <u>joy</u>, <u>goodness</u> ...*

**The Bible**

*The* third and final avenue or "branch" through which love will channel itself is "Reverence". This "branch" affects your relationship with your Creator and the spirit realm (see Illus. 22–1).

When your *emotional*-self is free of wounding, pain, fear, depression and anger, it is free to experience love. It is free to receive love. It is free to give love. As this is taking place within your heart or *emotional*-self, you find that you have a deeper sense of love, respect, reverence and even an awe toward your Creator and the spirit realm. Your spiritual senses heighten. Your love and devotion toward your Creator increases. You find yourself enjoying, on an *emotional* level, the luxuries and benefits of an emotionally close felt *connection* with your Creator. You feel a healthy respect and reverence toward the Creator of the universe. Your awe and respect for His loving interaction with

Illus. 22–1: **Reverence: The Third Branch**

humanity, and specifically with you personally, replaces a felt distance or lack of reverence toward heavenly things.

At this point, this heavenly relationship becomes comfortable for you. You feel much more relaxed and at peace with your Creator. A deep, inner acceptance of His love, devotion and commitment for your life replaces any fear of His wrath or punishment. You are able to view your Creator as a friend and close companion.

Fear of further wounding by God no longer haunts your heart. How can this be? It happens because you are free to receive and give love. As you are experiencing love you naturally desire to let your own love flow out of you and into others, including your Creator. You develop a life style of loving your Creator and desiring His presence.

When you are in this state of being, you grow into an awareness of the spirit-world and spiritual things. Your spirituality takes on a heightened or increased sense in your life. You make a deeper "connection" with the spirit-world. This connection transcends your humanity. Your senses pick up and perceive things that most people can't see. This happens simply because your spiritual senses are now much more alive. Your attention is not being consumed and distracted by emotional wounding, pain, fear, anger, rejection or depression. You are free to allow your spiritual senses to heighten and increase. You are free to feel and experience all that the spirit realm has to give and offer you and your spirit.

### The Fruit, or Outward Emotional Behavior

Once love is channeling itself through the avenue or "branch" of *reverence*, it culminates its journey within your *emotional*-self through external emotional behavior and feelings. These outward emotional behaviors and feelings are:

*faithfulness*,
*joy* and
*goodness* (see Illus. 22–2).

Illus. 22–2: **Faithfulness, Joy, Goodness: The Fruit**

In other words, as your emotions freely flow through all levels of your *emotional*-self, they ultimately culminate through your outward, external behavior. These external feelings and behaviors are *faithfulness, joy* and *goodness*. Notice that these three "fruits" are all felt emotions that you experience and express toward your Creator and the spirit-world. That is, when you experience a healthy reverence toward your Creator, you will experience:

greater measures of *faithfulness*,

greater measures of *joy*, and

greater measures of *goodness* toward your Creator and the spirit realm.

**Each of these emotional qualities directly relates to and affects your relationship with *your Creator and the spirit realm.*

### What are Faithfulness, Joy and Goodness?

Each of these three qualities is a felt emotion within your *emotional*-self. Specifically, though, how can you be aware of their presence or existence within your heart and life? To answer this question, you simply need to know and be aware of what these three "fruits" feel like when they are flowing in and through your *emotional*-self.

**1.** *Faithfulness* is an internal *commitment, dependence*, and *allegiance*, not only toward God, but also toward all other aspects and relationships in your life.

**2.** *Joy* is an internal *happiness, contentment, restfulness* and *peace.*

**3.** *Goodness* is an internal motivation of *humility, honesty, purity* and *truth.*

When you are whole, healed, free and at peace, *and* when you are feeling and experiencing a deep sense of *connection* within your life, your *emotional*-self produces each of these three "fruits" *effortlessly* and *naturally*. These three "fruits" are the *natural* emotional flow that manifests itself in your feelings and attitude toward your Creator and the spirit realm.

Can you see why, in order to feel and experience inner faithfulness, joy and goodness toward your Creator and the spirit-world, you have to begin by addressing the "root" or feelings of holiness?

So, now can you begin to see why we often fail when we try to put these qualities on ourselves like a suit of clothes? These qualities are produced from *within* because of the underlying "root" within us. We can not *acquire* these "fruits." We can only produce them, once the "root" of emotional holiness exists within our *emotional*-self.

These emotional "fruits" or external qualities are *not* experienced by attempting to focus on any other aspect of your *emotional*-self (other emotions that are progressively beyond the root or starting point, such as those in the trunk, branches, or fruit). You have to focus your energy on feeling and experiencing the root of *holiness*—wholeness and completeness—*emotionally*. This then, will ultimately produce the external "fruits" or feelings of peace, patience, self-control, love, gentleness, kindness, faithfulness, joy and goodness.

————— ◊ —————

*Remember & Reflect*     *1. The whole and healed **emotional**-self, once progressed to the stage of love, will manifest itself through three "branches," all of which spawn outward behaviors, or "fruits."*

*2. The third "branch" is Reverence, **toward your Creator** and the spirit realm.*

*3. This third "branch" or emotional response affects your relationship toward your Creator and the spirit realm.*

*4. Feelings of "Reverence" exist because of felt emotions of **love**, which trigger an awe or respect toward your Creator.*

5. This "branch" always produces outward behavior or "fruits" that, when left to themselves, will produce feelings and behavior of **faithfulness**, **joy** and **goodness**.

6. This feeling of reverence toward your Creator produces a desire and motivation to feel, build and develop a closer "**connection**" between you and your Creator and the spirit realm.

**The *Real*-Self**

# CHAPTER 23

# *Does This Really Work?*

## *A Review*

*D*oes this really work? Is it possible to experience genuine and permanent emotional love, healing, freedom and peace? Is it possible to change negative and destructive behavioral habits (mental, emotional, physical and verbal habits)?

Yes! It is very possible. To further encourage you in this hope, we want to share the stories of several who have experienced the effects of these principles first-hand as they each have walked through their own emotional Journey. None of these individuals are especially gifted in any way that is different from you or me. They, like you and I, are very normal, average people. There were no great giftings on their part, nor on the counselor's part, that allowed them to experience what they were needing. The stability and reliability of the principles involved, coupled with each person's willingness and desire to change, have caused their positive changes.

We trust their words will strengthen and encourage you.

**(words underscored by client)**

"My time with Life Institute has been one of the <u>best</u> experiences of my life. I am blessed that I was put in touch with Kevin and Mary. Because of their genuineness, loyalty, honesty, compassion, and hard work with me, I am fully aware of who I am and why I am here on this earth.

"When I first came to Life Institute I was a very confused, mixed up, but 'good' person. I could not understand my feelings and why I could not make decisions. I did not realize it then, but my self-confidence and self-esteem were very low. I lived my life basically out of fear and trying to gain acceptance from others.

"During the weeks spent going through the counseling process, I began to feel a sense of <u>peace</u> and harmony entering my life. I felt myself getting <u>stronger</u> and <u>stronger</u> every day. I followed the instructions and put a lot of hard work and effort into the assignments that were given to me and I began to know myself, trust myself and change for the good. I loved the uniqueness of the process. There was a true beginning and end. I felt progress was always being made after each week. The process was not just "going to therapy week after week" and feeling no end result. Kevin gets to the "heart" of the matter, and helps you get in touch with yourself. He helps you to know yourself, and then helps you truly change from within.

"Since having completed the process, I feel, for the first time, at the age of 35, I have <u>just</u> <u>begun</u> to live my life! My life is full of peace, joy and contentment. My self-confidence and self-esteem are very high, and I <u>love</u> <u>myself</u> and I <u>love</u> <u>life</u>! I have learned to conquer my fears and stand up to them. I have learned to deal with problems and hurdles in a very constructive manner. I have taken <u>responsibility</u> for <u>myself</u>.

"Kevin & Mary, you both deserve to be <u>greatly</u> blessed. What you do for others can permanently change an individual for the better. I feel very blessed that you entered my life.

"Thank you for <u>making</u> a <u>difference</u>!"

C. S.
Plano, TX

*******

"Before I went to Life Institute Counseling my life was full of fear. I was afraid of making any kind of decision for fear of *rejection, fear of failure, and just fear of being wrong. I would pray long periods of time before I did anything and still I was paralyzed with fear of making the wrong decision.*

*"Through counseling I learned there are no wrong decisions. A situation not turning out for the best is only a learning experience. Hesitation and not making a decision at all are the only wrong decisions because they are based out of fear.*

*"Now my life is so different. Each day I am trying to make as many decisions as possible. I have peace, joy, and an excitement in my life because I have learned, and am still learning how to conquer fear and not let it control me.*

*"Thank you Kevin and Mary!"*

B. S.<br>Dallas, TX

*******

*"Before I started counseling with Kevin Turner, my life was miserable. I basically hated everything about my life. One of my favorite songs was 'Comfortably Numb' by Pink Floyd. This song summed up my life. Because I couldn't face the pain, depression, and hurt. I resorted to alcohol and whatever vice I could get my hands on. So, thus I became 'Comfortably Numb.' One of the lines in the song said, 'Your lips move but I can't hear what you're saying.' I sought help from churches, or anyone who seemed that they might have some answers. I even had prayer sessions over me in hopes of relieving the pain. I got temporary relief from prayers but any counsel or 'words of wisdom' was to no avail. Truly, all well meaning counselors lips did move. But I just couldn't <u>hear</u> what they were saying.*

*"What I have realized during and after my counseling is that I have control over the way I feel. I don't have to resort to any self-destructive vices anymore. And because I am in control, I can do anything I set my mind to. I have also realized that I have specific gifts that God has given me and He has some specific things that He wants me to accomplish while on this earth. I have just written a song and the chorus is,*

*" 'I want to be there for you, just like*
*you've been there for me.*
*'I want to hear your every heart beat, not*
*for the honor of men,*
*'Just to be your friend.*

*'I just want to be there for you.'*

"*It's true. I want to be there for my Creator. I want to hear His heartbeat. I want to be His best friend.*

"*I would like to say that life now is easy and rosy. The pain inside has greatly diminished. But what I have learned is that some days are a battle and I have to fight for my peace. My life now is 100% better. I know that I still have a ways to go but I am not walking in ignorance anymore. I now have the tools and the knowledge to walk in peace, to experience love, and to be happy.*

"*I know that life isn't easy. You have to work at it. But once you begin to experience its victories there is no turning back.*"

T. M.

Sacramento, CA.

*******

"*For my entire life, I had been a people pleaser and as the years went by, I began to realize that I was angry at always doing what others wanted, but never seeming to do what I truly desired. I was fortunate to grow up in a home with both parents who loved me very much. But I suffered from insecurity, perceived rejection, constant internalized criticism, and an unreasonable desire for perfection.*

"*As I went through the process at Life Institute, I began to experience how my life became more simplified and enjoyable than I would have ever imagined or thought possible. One of my initial concerns going into counseling was that I often felt that I had no feelings. I would go for long periods of time, feeling that I had no emotions whatsoever, punctuated with shorter, but intense periods of total anger and frustration. Through the process at Life Institute, I was given a combination of powerful, yet simple tools and steps to deal with my emotions on a daily, and even hourly basis. As the process continued, a real wholeness and freshness developed in both my attitude and outlook on life. In fact, towards the end of my time at Life Institute, I received a much better job opportunity and working environment. I believe that this opportunity was due, in large part, to my coming to grips with who I was and what I wanted out of life through my sessions at Life Institute.*

"*There were also a lot of issues I had to deal with in my past including unfulfilled expectations and unresolved emotions. In addition, I had difficulties dealing with my immediate family.*

*There was even a two-year time period in adolescence where I became anorexic and experienced at least three instances in my life where my life almost ended. I am so thankful that the Lord intervened in my life, and so glad that Kevin Turner offered me a process, through Life Institute, where I could get my life back together again and begin to live an exciting and successful life that I had never dreamed before would be possible.*

*"I would encourage anyone who wishes to take charge of their life to get involved in the process at Life Institute. An acceleration of events occurs in your life as you begin to put into action and practice the tools and techniques presented. There are no magic steps, but as you commit to the process, you will see amazing things begin to take place in all aspects and facets of your life."*

J. B.
Lewisville, TX

\*\*\*\*\*\*\*

The wife:

*"I was at a very low point before my husband and I began to receive counseling from Kevin. In ways I felt hopeless for myself and our marriage as our communication had gotten to a point that so much misunderstanding had pulled us apart. In addition to this, I was concerned about our girls' future, with us constantly at odds with one another.*

*"When we were going to the Life Institute on a regular basis, I felt relief. I knew we were being cared for and that our sessions were "tailor made" for our situation. It was hard work, some phases were painful, but the end result truly taught me how to choose joy in everyday life. I learned that I am an emotional being and can have control over my feelings.*

*"Our time at LICS has certainly been life changing for me. I reflect often on the time we invested and I view my life differently now. I focus on my personal relationship with my Heavenly Father daily like I never have in my life. The Biblical foundations that Kevin planted in me, I feel, are a permanent, lasting part of my life. I think before I communicate now and the tension in our marriage is virtually gone. We do not let issues build up and continue to pull us down or draw us away from each other.*

*"I know my husband and I are on the same side now and the freedom to love each other keeps growing. Now, it all seems so simple to reflect on the basics Kevin revealed to us. It is flowing into my entire life on how I view things. Thank you Lord for using Kevin in our life and helping to heal our marriage!"*

The husband:

*"Before coming to LICS, the relationship with my wife, was like that of walking on eggshells. We were frequently hurting each other's feelings.*

*"During the weeks of counsel, I felt like a pioneer; definitely new territory, individually and as a couple, was addressed during our sessions. A major step, much to my surprise, was confronting fears and seeing them dissolve. I have incorporated this into my everyday life. The healing and the strengthening was worth the hard work and time involved. I am finding these new approaches/attitudes are a permanent part of my life too.*

*"Since completing the sessions, I know my wife trusts my love for her. This has inspired me to demonstrate my love for my wife in different ways. I realize my faith in God is essential. Thanks be to God for His indescribable gift! (II Corinthians 9:15)"*

> S.&M. A.
> Dallas, TX

*******

*"We were desperate when we came to Life Institute. Both of us are very emotionally strong individuals. But all of our efforts to deal with our problems had not worked. I felt life really was not worth living. I honestly hoped that I would not wake up some morning. At least then, the nightmare would be over.*

*"Our first meeting was a little disconcerting. The approach seemed much too simple to us. We had very complicated problems that needed solutions equally as complicated. Everyone thinks their problems are unique and worse than everyone else's. The idea that we could work through them in just 20 weeks or so seemed so ridiculous.*

*"We discovered just the opposite. We began to see results almost immediately. The process is specific in design for each person. It unfolds naturally as one follows the guidelines. But*

*you do have to be committed to doing the work, and it is intense. However, the rewards are real and worth it!*

*"Unlike many counseling programs that just keep you coming back and cause you to become dependent on the counselor, Life Institute's approach deals with your immediate problems and teaches you how to live a fuller, happier life in the future by following the steps <u>on your own</u>.*

*"The bottom line is that Life Institute's approach is a simple, practical one, that, when diligently applied, works."*

D.&P. S.
Plano, TX

\*\*\*\*\*\*\*

*"At the time I started in counseling with Kevin and Mary Turner, I was at a crisis time in my life. It was brought on by events I had no control over. My husband had just filed for divorce and I was left feeling hopeless, deeply grieved and totally bewildered. Each time I went to counseling, I came away encouraged, with a sense that at last I was getting real help for emotional difficulties I was experiencing.*

*"I had looked for answers for years as to how to get rid of unhealthy emotional baggage that I knew was preventing me from enjoying and experiencing life to its fullest. I read books, listened to sermons, talked to friends that seemed to have it all together. Whatever I thought might help, I tried. But nothing really seemed to help me.*

*"But counseling with Kevin and Mary was a life changing experience for me. They coached me in what I needed to deal with and how to effectively resolve issues that were hindering me. I have never been happier and am now having the fun and joy that for years I knew I was missing out on. I now have more wonderful, healthy relationships than I have ever had in my life, without working hard for them. They just happen naturally. It still amazes me.*

*"It has been many months now since I finished counseling, and life just keeps getting better. My counseling experience was not a temporary fix, but a true healing of what was causing my difficulties, so that now I can grow and blossom to be what God had intended for me to be all along."*

S. K., M.D.
Dallas, TX

*******

The Wife:

*"When I started at Life Institute I was so depressed. I felt lonely, bitter, angry, ashamed, and most of all, so full of <u>guilt</u>. With the guidance of the Life Institute, I found the Key to my feelings and problems. Through the counseling I experienced love and forgiveness. I began experiencing peace on a regular basis. The peace began relieving me of all the guilt. This was the biggest factor for me during that time of counseling.*

*"Since having completed counseling, I am happier today than ever before. My heart floods with thankfulness to be able to feel love and forgiveness, no matter how deep the problem.*

*"Our praise to God for two special people who cared and understood our feelings - Kevin & Mary Turner."*

S. P.

Highland Park, TX

The Husband:

*"When I first called Life Institute, I was desperate yet determined. I knew our marriage was in serious trouble. However, I knew that our marriage could be restored and repaired if both my wife and I would agree to be open, truthful, and work at it together.*

*"Kevin gave me what would turn out to be the greatest advice I have ever received. It was a principle of conduct that, to this day, I still apply to my relationship with my wife.*

*"As a result, God began to supernaturally repair and restore our marriage to what He had intended it to be.*

*"During the weeks spent in counseling, Kevin and Mary helped my wife and I determine the root of our problems. I found that my lack of trust, and fear of losing my wife had hurt my marriage through the years, and that this fear eventually was coming true. Through counseling, the Lord helped me overcome my fears, giving me confidence and trust in my wife that I had never had before.*

*"It has been almost two years since my wife and I completed our counseling at Life Institute. During this time God has healed my wife and me by removing her guilt and anger, and*

*my fear and lack of trust. Today, our marriage is strong and driven by a deep and faithful love and trust for each other."*
T. P.
Highland Park, TX

\*\*\*\*\*\*\*

*"I turned to the services of Life Institute after I realized my life just could not go on the way it was. I was miserably unhappy and depressed, even though I seemed to have it all; an adoring husband, a beautiful child, and a loving home. I wouldn't let others get close to me, even though I desperately wanted close relationships. I felt alone, unloved, and unwanted by the world. I also had a very unhealthy image of God and thought I could never be worthy of love in His eyes, because of the awful things I had done. I thought I had to be perfect, and so I gave every outward appearance of having attained perfection. I thought that no one would like the real me, if they were to know the real me, so I spent a lot of time being someone else. It finally got to the point where I just could not go on doing that anymore. I was so unhappy I wanted to die.*

*"The first time I met Kevin Turner was the first time I actually experienced hope, however guarded, that my life could be changed. I started doing all of the assignments, which seemed monumental at first, and began to see a pattern to my behavior. What happened during the six months I spent in counseling will forever be with me. I was able to let go of all the fearful thoughts that had controlled me. I was able to love others and myself, unconditionally. I discovered who I really am and my purpose in life. The wounds of childhood and beyond were finally understood and healed.*

*"I can honestly say that I am a happy, joyous person now. My life has purpose and meaning. I know where I am going with my life. My relationships have become so beautiful and loving since going through counseling at Life Institute. I like the person that I am and shall never be ashamed of who I am again. I live the life of love now, that had previously seemed like a distant fantasy. I am living proof that it can happen. My life will never be the same (praise God) because of the help I received from Life Institute. "*
P. L.
Flower Mound, TX

# *Review*
## Part III

A review "Part III: The Other Side of Life":

**Chapter Fifteen:**

## *Holiness: The Root*
### *The Other Side of Life*

1. The *emotional-self* is a multi-level, multi-sectioned entity within all of us.
2. Emotional fruit is *produced*, *not* acquired.
3. Within your *real*-self (the whole and healed you), the emotional "*root*" of your *emotional*-self is *holiness*.
4. Holiness is emotional *wholeness* and *completeness*.
5. *Five keys* stimulate and produce a felt sense of holiness:

> 1. Emotional *control*,
> 2. A felt sense of *connection*,
> 3. A healthy *attitude*,
> 4. Emotional *healing*, and
> 5. Self-identification or *purpose*.

**Chapter Sixteen:**

## *Hope: The Trunk*
### *The Other Side of Life*

1. Feeling *holiness*—wholeness and completeness—emotionally, causes you to feel feelings of hope.
2. Hope is an *internal optimism* that you feel toward yourself, your life and your future.
3. Hope is to your heart what an anchor is to a ship: an emotional protector from life's treacheries. Hope is an anchor for your soul (the mind, will and emotions).
4. Holiness produces *hope*.
5. This process is *emotional*, not physical, mental or spiritual, in nature. However, it almost always will affect the mental, physical and spiritual areas of our lives. It is an *emotional* process that controls your feelings and attitudes. These feelings and attitudes, repeatedly felt and experienced often enough, eventually become behavioral *habits*.

**Chapter Seventeen:**

## Faith:  The Trunk
### The Other Side of Life

**1**. A felt sense of *connection* produces feelings of *holiness*—wholeness and completeness—*emotionally.*

**2**. Holiness produces *hope.*

**3**. Hope produces *faith.*

**4**. Faith is more than trust or belief.  It is *risk-taking.*  It can only come if you *first* feel hope, which is an *internal* emotional feeling of *optimism* that you feel toward yourself and your life.

**5**. This process is emotional, not physical, mental or spiritual.  However, it almost always affects the mental, physical and spiritual areas of your life. It is an emotional process that controls your feelings and attitudes.  These feelings and attitudes, repeatedly felt and experienced often enough, eventually become behavioral habits,

**Chapter Eighteen:**

## Love:  The Trunk
### The Other Side of Life

**1**. Emotional expressions of faith (optimism and *risk-taking*) cause, trigger or produce felt feelings of *love.*

**2**. Love is powerful enough to conquer and control fear.

**3**. Love is *unconditional giving* and *acceptance.*

**4**. Love is an *emotion* and an *attitude.*  It is not merely an action.  Actions and words of love are fruits of genuine, felt love living within the heart

**Chapter Nineteen:**

## Whole, Healed Outward Behavior:  The Fruit
### The Other Side of Life

**1**. Just as the wounded-self produces outward behavior, or "fruit," so also, the real-self produces "fruit."

**2**. The "fruit" of the real-self is peace, patience, self-control, love, gentleness, kindness, faithfulness, joy and goodness.

**3**. These nine emotional qualities are "branched," or channeled through three basic areas, or realms of relationship in each of our lives.

**Chapter Twenty:**

## *Responsibility: The First Branch*
### *The Other Side of Life*

1. The whole and healed emotional-self, once progressed to the stage of love, will manifest itself through three "branches," all of which spawn outward behaviors, or "fruits."
2. The first "branch" is "Responsibility," personally,.
3. This "branch" is directed toward *your self.*
4. These feelings of "Responsibility" exist because you are in control and in charge of who you are, how you feel and for the circumstances in your life.
5. This "branch" of emotional responsibility always produces outward behaviors or "fruits" that, when left to themselves, will produce feelings and behavior of *peace, patience and self-control.*
6. When left unbridled and uncontrolled, this emotional "fruit" inevitably builds and enhances healthy self-confidence, self-esteem and self-value. It produces self-affirmed living, not self-focused or selfish living.

**Chapter Twenty-One:**

## *Respect: The Second Branch*
### *The Other Side of Life*

1. The whole and healed emotional-self, your *real*-self, once progressed to the stage of love, will manifest itself through three "branches," all of which spawn outward behaviors, or "fruits."
2. The second "branch" is "Respect," toward others.
3. This "branch" affects your relationship with others around you.
4. These feelings of "Respect" exist because of felt emotions of *love*, which trigger an ability to *trust* others.
5. This "branch" of emotional *respect* always produces outward behavior or "fruits" that, when left to themselves, will produce feelings and behavior of *love, gentleness* and *kindness.*
6. When left unbridled and uncontrolled, this emotional "fruit" inevitably builds and enhances healthy, successful friendships and relationships.

**Chapter Twenty-Two:**

## *Reverence: The Third Branch*
### *The Other Side of Life*

1. The whole and healed emotional-self, once progressed to the stage of love, will manifest itself through three "branches," all of which spawn outward behaviors, or "fruits."

2. The third "branch" is "Reverence," *toward your Creator and the spirit world.*
3. This third "branch" or emotional response affects your relationship toward your Creator and the spirit world.
4. These feelings of "Reverence" exist because of felt emotions of *love*, which trigger an awe, respect or reverence toward your Creator.
5. This "branch" of emotional reverence always produces outward behavior or "fruits" that, when left  to themselves, will produce feelings and behavior of *faithfulness, joy* and *goodness.*
6. This feeling of reverence toward your Creator produces a desire and motivation to feel build, and develop a closer "*connection*" between you and your Creator and the spirit world.

# The *Real*-Self

# CONCLUDING THOUGHTS

# *Hang-ups and Hindrances*

*A*side from our ignorance or misunderstanding of the laws and principles that govern the *emotional*-self, additional hang-ups and hindrances to our emotional healing and happiness sometimes exist. Most of these hang-ups and hindrances usually involve a preoccupation or distraction with one of the other three realms of our lives: mentally, physically or spiritually.

### Mentally
When a person tries to *first* gain an *intellectual* understanding of how the emotional process works, he or she usually runs into a lot of difficulty. Why? Because there are some things which must first be experienced *within the heart* before they can be understood. Those who have experienced Divine encounters or spiritual experiences understand this concept fully well. The same is true for those who wish to experience emotional healing, change and self-improvement within their *emotional*-self. *Emotions must be experienced before they can be understood.*

However, this does not mean that we must trash the mind and all intellectual understanding. On the contrary. It just simply means that the mind can only function within its governing laws or perimeters. As such, the mind is limited when it comes to experiential living. The heart or *emotional*-self is designed for experiential living. The mind is not.

Most of us are entrenched in believing that our emotions and feelings are all in our minds. They are not. As we learned in Chapter Two, our *emotional*-self is a completely separate entity from our mental, psychological or intellectual self. Again, this is why psychological tools and principles do not generally produce genuine, permanent and long-lasting change and healing for the heart or *emotional*-self.

In addition to this, you may have a difficult time believing that the answer to emotional healing and change could be this simple. After all, you have been plagued with your fear, anger, depression or wounding for much of your life. You have already tried everything you know, without long-lasting results or satisfaction. So, it is easy to understand why you would be skeptical that this could really work.

For those who would say—

*"This is too simplistic. It can not be this easy."*—

Remember that some of the greatest discoveries throughout history, whether physical/scientific, or philosophical/religious in nature, were often overlooked for centuries because of their simplicity. Many discoveries have been found to be very simple, once their mysteries were uncovered and understood. The same is true for our emotions and feelings.

*Many things in life are simple, yet profound.* This is the case with our *emotional*-self and the principles that govern it. Once understood, it is found to be simple and predictable, yet profound. But do not necessarily take our word for it. Put these principles to the test. See for yourself.

**Physically**

Our physical lives can hinder us in our quest for emotional wholeness and healing, as well. Our physical environment, our friends, and our job atmosphere can each hinder our hearts and hold us back from experiencing all that life should offer us. As we learned in previous chapters, we can do all of the right, proper and correct things emotionally and still stay bogged down, *if* our physical environment is a negative detriment to our heart-nature.

**Spiritually**

After reading this book, you may ask,

*"Isn't this Journey more spiritual than emotional?"*

I don't think so. I have had many spiritual experiences. But, they are different experientially from the emotional Journey discussed in this book. However, when comparing the spiritual experiences with the emotional ones, I have learned that the spiritual life is *enhanced* by a whole and healed *emotional*-self. The spiritual life does *not replace* the *emotional*-self, nor is it the *emotional*-self.

I have experienced six Divine encounters during my lifetime. They each were very different from the emotional experiences I feel and experience within my *emotional*-self.

However, one thing is very obvious to me. My Divine encounters and spiritual experiences have *conditioned* and *prepared* me for my own emotional Journey of emotional love, healing, freedom and peace. The spiritual life *propelled* and *compelled* me to pursue my own emotional healing and enter into my own emotional Journey out of wounding and into love, healing, freedom and peace.

The Journey itself is not spiritual, in nature, although the spiritual realm definitely affects and influences one's emotional Journey.

**Concluding Words**

This book is an attempt to explain, in a simplistic illustration of two trees, *why* we are who we are *emotionally,* and what we can do in our present and future lives to enjoy this life we have. Many of us are wounded and hurting. We are not weak, inferior, mentally sick, crazy, or psychotic— just wounded. This book is an attempt to help us understand why we *do* some of the things we do, *say* some of the things we say, *think* some of the things we think, and *feel* some of the things we feel. In short, I hope that this book will help you understand and get in touch with the *real* you—your *emotional*-self.

There are many, many principles in the Bible that shed light on the emotional issues which we face in our lives. We have only touched on a small fraction of those principles in this book. All of these principles are additional windows of understanding into who we are, how we feel and what our purpose is in life. I encourage you to pursue the answers to your life's issues from within the Bible; not necessarily for direct, quick answers, but for the inspiration and insight that will lead and direct you to the answers. Seek those windows. They are rich opportunities for you. Don't stop until you have accomplished the quest, *emotionally.*

*Learn to listen to your entire being:*  mentally, physically, spiritually, as well as emotionally. *What is it telling you?* Accept what it is telling you and abide in it. If your being warns you, heed the warning. If it encourages you, follow its lead. If your heart has peace, proceed. If your peace is stolen, retrace and back up. Life can be that simple, *if you will only listen to your heart.*

Learn to follow your heart.

It will serve you well.

Kevin Lane Turner

# Glossary of Terms

**Abuse:** To misuse or use wrongly with excessiveness.

**Alienation:** Real or perceived, felt isolation, loneliness, rejection.

**Anger:** Pent-up feelings of being wronged or violated.

**Anomaly:** Abnormal.

**Anxiety:** Worry or uneasiness that to an extreme will trigger panic, stress, tension or fear.

**Attitude:** A mental approach or perspective toward self, life, God or others.

**Authorities:** Parental, vocational and spiritual figures designed to govern, lead, and guide our lives.

**Behavioral Habit Life Style:** Thoughts, words, actions and feelings that are common to your ever-day experience.

**Bitterness:** A felt hard harshness toward self, life, God or others.

**Body:** The physical shell encasing the human entity.

**Branch:** A channel or avenue—the means by which something moves or is carried.

**Channel:** See "Branch."

**Complex:** Consisting of a number of hard-to-understand parts.

**Compliance:** To please and appease others at the expense of one's own heart-nature in an attempt to avoid conflict or rejection.

**Confusion:** A disordered mix up.

**Connection/connectedness:** The felt sense of being joined together.

**Control:** Exerting power, authority or direction.

**Correlation:** A mutual relation, connection or similarity between two things.

**Defiling the Flesh:** External emotional behavior–fruit–that inevitably can and will destroy the mental, emotional, physical or spiritual parts of a person's life.

**Deliverance:** A spiritual process or exercise of freeing or releasing a person from negative and destructive influences—demons, habits, memories, etc.

**Depression/depressive behavior:** A sinking, lowering, pressing down feeling. It is a feeling of hopelessness, no say–so, no-control, over who you are, how you feel, or for the circumstances surrounding your life.

**Detrimental:** Harmful or injurious loss or damage.

**Emotions:** One of four parts of our human entity. The "feeling" part of the human entity that produces and houses your fears and feelings.

**Emotional chain reaction:** The process of one emotional feeling reacting off of a previous one, repeatedly and consecutively.

**Emotional control:** See "Control."

**Emotional expectations**: Spoken and non spoken hopes, desires or preferences one places on another, in hopes of feeling better, happier or more fulfilled.

**Emotional healing**: The felt experience of being whole, free and at peace emotionally.

**Emotional irresponsibility:** An attitude of looking to, hoping in, blaming and holding responsible, other people, situations or God for who you are, how you feel, or for the circumstances in your life.

**Emotional savior**: See "Emotional Irresponsibility."

**Emotional suicide**: The cutting off or death of the good, healthy and positive feelings intended for the human creation from birth.

**Emotional-self**: The emotional part of our human entity.

**Encasement**: A wall of protection.

**Encroachment**: Uninvited intrusion, invasion or trespass.

**Entity**: The *whole* of the human existence.

**Etymology**: The study of words.

**Euphemism**: The substitution of one word by another which is softer or milder in meaning.

**External environment**: Your physical surroundings.

**Faith**: Believing that something, in which you can not see, will happen or occur.

**Faithfulness**: An internal commitment, dependence or allegiance, not only toward God, but also toward all other aspects and relationships in one's life.

**Fear**: Believing that something which you can not see will happen or occur.

**Fear of rejection**: A felt feeling or premonition, either real or perceived, of being alienated or unaccepted.

**Fear-based life style**: A life style or behavior pattern dictated by real or imagined fear.

**Ferret**: The process of investigating or searching out.

**Fruit**: External behaviors: mental, emotional, verbal and physical behaviors.

**Gentleness**: A soft, tender, compassion toward those around you. It carries with it an understanding for the circumstances of others.

**Goodness**: An internal motivation of humility, honesty, purity and truth.

**Habit**: A mental, emotional, physical or verbal activity that is subconsciously performed, executed or carried out, consistently.

**Habitat**: The physical place of abode, residence or existence.

**Head-based**: Intellectually based, focused or derived.

**Healing**: See "Emotional Healing."

**Healthy attitude**: An attitude and perspective toward self, life, God, and others which produces attitudes and feelings of love, peace, joy, freedom and understanding.

**Heart**: Your *emotional*-self.

**Heart of God**: The emotional side of our Creator.

**Heart of man**: In this book this refers to the wounded-self. See "Wounded-Self."

**Heart-based**: Emotionally based, focused or derived.

**Heart-nature**: The instinctive emotional nature of man and woman. Your whole, healed and complete *emotional*-self, apart from wounding.

**Holiness**: A felt sense of wholeness and completeness.

**Hope**: An internal optimism toward yourself and your life.

**Hopelessness**: The absence of hope.

**Ingrained**: Solidly or firmly planted or rooted.

**Interdependent**: Mutual need or dependence.

**Interrelated**: Mutual connection or association.

**Internal emotional reactionary process**: See ""Emotional Chain Reaction."

**Internal optimism**: Internally felt hope and promise.

**Invader**: See "Encroachment."

**Iron Claws Process**: One aspect of the Life Institute counseling/life improvement process that rids an individual of all unhealthy, unfilled emotional expectations and the subsequent emotional pain that accompanies those expectations.

**Isolation**: The felt sense of being alone.

**Joy**: An internal happiness, contentment, restfulness and peace.

**Journey/the journey**: **a.**) A change in thought, approach and *perception from* the mental, physical or spiritual, to the emotional perspective of life.

**Journey/the journey**: **b.**) A reference to a process of experiencing emotional love, healing, freedom and peace.

**Kindness**: An open willingness to accept others for who they are and where they are in life.

**Lack of Respect:** The opposite of respect—see "Respect".

**Lack of Responsibility:** The opposite of responsibility—see "Responsibility".

**Lack of Reverence:** The opposite of reverence—see "Reverence."

**Life Improvement**: The process of changing one's life and life style by changing and altering one's emotions.

**Loneliness**: See "Isolation" and "Alienation."

**Love**: Unconditional giving and acceptance toward life and others.

**Masked life:** The life style projection of who we want to be or how we want others to see us.

**Mental**: One of four parts of our human entity. The "thinking" part of the human entity. It is your psyche and houses your mind and it's thoughts.

**Metamorphosis**: A noticeable change in form, make-up, or structure.

**Mind/will**: Your psychological being, your intellect.

**Morbidity**: An unhealthy, sickly, diseased condition.

**Other side of Life**: Life lived in emotional wholeness, freedom, peace and love; as opposed to life lived with the familiar fears, feelings, wounds and pain.

**Patience**: An internal willingness to restfully wait.

**Peace**: An internal, restful contentment and pleasure that you feel toward yourself and your life.

**Perception**: How one takes in, interprets and processes the externals in his or her life.

**Perfection**: The inclination, drive or compulsion to be and perform in a spotless, blameless, perfect manner.

**Performance-based living**: A life style of activity based on the consumed desire and ambition to *feel* (not be) loved, accepted, valued or needed.

**Performance oriented living**: See "Performance-based living.

**Personal attitude**: See "Attitude."

**Pessimism**: Internal, felt feelings of fear, doubt, dread or impending doom.

**Phenomenon**: An extraordinary or exceptional event or circumstance that can be observed.

**Plantar wart:** A wart, caused by a virus, which attaches itself to your outer flesh and roots tentacles through your skin, into your body.

**Plethora**: An overabundance.

**Propagate**: The act of reproducing.

**Psychotherapy**: The practice of psychology—the study of the mind.

**Purity**: The felt emotion of cleanliness.

**Purpose**: An intended plan, aim, desire or ambition.

**React/reaction**: Voluntarily or involuntarily responding to an action.

**Reactive**: See "React."

**Real heart:** The whole, healed and free *emotional*-self.

**Realm**: An area, region, or sphere.

**Real-self:** See "Real heart."

**Rebellion**: A resistant, defensive, pushing away for defensive, protective purposes, emotionally.

**Rejecting authority:** An inability or refusal to trust others, especially authorities in one's life.

**Respect**: A peaceful trust and regard for others and their boundaries.

**Responsibility**: Being in control and in charge of who you are, how you feel, and for the circumstances surrounding your life.

**Reverence**: An internal feeling of respect toward God and the things of God.

**Reviling angelic majesties**: A mocking or indifference toward God and the spirit realm.

**Root**: The deepest, inner-most core of your *emotional*-self.

**Self-affirmed living**: Exerting influence and control in every facet of your life to the degree that every aspect of your life (job, relationships, etc.) affirms you and who you are.

**Self-centeredness:** A consumed focus and preoccupation with yourself, your feelings, your fears, your image, etc., usually for the purposes of self-protection and self-preservation, emotionally.

**Self-control:** See "Responsibility."

**Self-denial**: The act and process of discounting, doubting and denying one's own ability, intuition, instincts and personhood in order to be accepted and not rejected.

**Self-discovery:** The activity of realizing who you are, why you are here and where you are going, mentally, emotionally, physically, relationally and spiritually.

**Self-identification/purpose**: See "Self-discovery."

**Self-nature**: See "Heart-nature."

**Self-preservation:** The activity and focus of preserving yourself, mentally, emotionally and physically.

**Self-protection:** The activity and focus of protecting yourself, mentally, emotionally and physically.

**Shift**: A change in direction or thinking.

**Spirit**: a.) The inner-most part of the *emotional*-self which gives you the zeal and motivation for life and living.

**Spirit**: b.) One of four aspects, or parts, of the human entity. The part of you which allows you to know and perceive the existence of your Creator.

**Spiritual**: One of four parts of our human entity. It is the part that allows an individual to know, perceive and be connected with his or her Creator and the spirit realm.

**Stress**: Emotional overload and extreme emotional pressure.

**Tree**: The figurative picture of your *emotional*-self.

**Trigger**: External variables that set off or stimulate our fears, feelings and emotions.

**Trust**: The ability to risk or believe in another outside of yourself.

**Unconditional acceptance**: The ability to receive another without first changing them to meet your preference.

**Unconditional giving**: Dispensing verbal, mental and physical acts of love and kindness, without measuring merit.

**Unconditional love and acceptance**: Verbal, mental and physical giving and receiving, without measuring merit.

**Unfulfilled emotional expectations:** See "Emotional expectations."

**Wounded heart:** See "Wounded-self."

**Wounded spirit:** The "root" hurt or pain that destructively transforms and changes your *emotional*-self.

**Wounded-self**: The wounded *emotional*-self.

**Wounding**: Emotional hurt and pain experienced within the heart or *emotional*-self.

# Illustration Index

*Chapter fourteen uses the tree illustrations of chapters seven through
  thirteen to depict three real-life scenerios.

# Bible Verse Index

**Note**:

To find any Bible verse referenced in *A Journey to the Other Side of Life*, break the below references into three parts as follows:

example: **Genesis 1:26**

1) **Genesis** — Looking in the contents page at the front of your Bible, you will find the page number in your Bible where this particular "**book**" of the Bible begins (the names are referred to as "books" and not chapter titles).

2) **1:** — This number refers to the **chapter** where the Bible reference can be found. In this case the Bible reference is found in the "**book**" of Genesis, **chapter** one.

3) **:26** — This number refers to the **verse** where the Bible reference is found. In our example, the Bible reference is found in **verse** 26.

# INDEX

279

# About the Author

Kevin Lane Turner counsels, writes and speaks in the field of emotions as it pertains to personal life-improvement, relationships, life's purpose and spirituality. He has almost twenty years experience as an educator, counselor and minister.

Childhood experiences of emotional emptiness, pain and wounding instilled within Kevin a search for answers as to the *whys* of human emotional behavior and a discovery of emotional wholeness, healing and fulfillment. Having developed an emotionally focused technique for counseling and life-improvement, Kevin is the founder and director of Life Institute, a center for emotionally focused counseling and life-improvement. He is also the president of the non-profit Family Life Counseling Institute.

He has a BA degree and a Masters degree in Divinity. Kevin is also a member of Who's Who Worldwide, a registry of global business leaders. He resides in Dallas, Texas with his wife of sixteen years and their six children.

Kevin is currently working on the sequel to *A Journey to the Other Side of Life*, which details Phase I of the life-improvement process.

If unavailable in local bookstores, additional copies of this and other publications by Kevin Lane Turner may be purchased by writing or calling the publisher at:

Ashley Down Publishing Company
14999 Preston Rd, Suite D212-222
Dallas, TX  75240-7811
(214) 233-9998

# About Life Institute

The Life Institute counseling/life-improvement process walks an individual or couple through an emotional transformation. It is a transformation away from the behaviors, habits and experiences depicted in Part II of this book —"the wounded-self"—, and into the experiences depicted in Part III—"the real-self".

This process changes:

> A. your day-in and day-out *habits* and *behavior*,
>
> B. the way you *feel*, day-in and day-out.
>
> (these two ultimately control your success in relationships, vocation and lifestyle.)

These changes are accomplished through a process of:

1. Personal empowerment and responsibility—mentally, emotionally, verbally, and physically— in the following areas:
   a. over negative/detrimental thoughts, feelings, words, and actions,
   b. over negative/detrimental behavioral habits, and
   c. over your life, lifestyle, relationships, your future direction and your purpose.
2. Understanding why you are the way you are behaviorally and emotionally:
   a. discovering the influence of past, painful wounding experiences within your own personal behavior and habits,
   b. how those past emotionally painful experiences have held you back and hindered your life, relationships, and your self-concept,
   c. facing the past—not to sit and soak in it, but in order to eliminate its power and influence over your present and future life.
3. Moving forward with life and eliminating the power, sting, and negative influence of the past and its detrimental influence on your current behavior, habits, relationships, and lifestyle.
4. Getting in touch with the real you:
   a. who you really are—apart from fear, wounding, and the negative habit patterns they have caused within your life.
   b. why you are on this planet—discovering your purpose in life, and
   c. where you are headed with your future—goals and direction.
5. Developing a lifestyle of vision, direction, and purpose.
6. Developing a lifestyle of emotional and relational wholeness, healing, freedom, and peace.
7. Developing an ability to pleasurably communicate and relate with those around you.

For more information about this life-improvement process, you may call or write:
Family Life Counseling Institute
Dallas North Parkway
P.O. Box 116
Addison, TX 75001

284